STORMS WILL TELL

JANET FRAME

Storms Will Tell

SELECTED POEMS

BLOODAXE BOOKS

ISBN: 978 1 85224 789 8

First published 2008 by
Bloodaxe Books Ltd,
Highgreen,
Tarset,
Northumberland NE48 1RP.

www.bloodaxebooks.com
For further information about Bloodaxe titles
please visit our website or write to
the above address for a catalogue.

Bloodaxe Books Ltd acknowledges
the financial assistance of
Arts Council England, North East.

ACKNOWLEDGEMENTS
Storms Will Tell reprints the whole of *The Goose Bath*
(Vintage/Random House, New Zealand, 2006), together with
a selection from *The Pocket Mirror* (George Braziller, Inc,
New York, 1967; W.H. Allen, London, 1968; Pegasus Press,
New Zealand, 1968; The Women's Press, London, 1992).

Cover design: Neil Astley & Pamela Robertson-Pearce.

Cover printing: J. Thomson Colour Printers Ltd, Glasgow.

Printed in Great Britain by
Bell & Bain Limited, Glasgow, Scotland.

CONTENTS

FROM *The Pocket Mirror* (1967)

JANET FRAME

Janet Frame was born in Dunedin, New Zealand, in 1924 into a working-class family. She was raised with a love of words, of literature and of nature, and her writing talent was recognised at an early age. However, writing, especially for a woman, was not regarded as a 'real job'.

The fate befalling the young woman who wanted 'to be a poet' has been well documented. Desperately unhappy because of family tragedies and finding herself trapped in the wrong vocation (as a schoolteacher), her only escape appeared to be in submission to society's judgement of her as abnormal. She spent four and a half years out of eight years incarcerated in mental hospitals. The story of her almost miraculous survival of the horrors and brutalising treatment in unenlightened institutions has become well known. She continued to write throughout her troubled years, and her first book (*The Lagoon and Other Stories*) won a prestigious literary prize, thus convincing her doctors not to carry out a planned lobotomy.

She returned to society, but not the one which had labelled her a misfit. She sought the support and company of fellow writers and set out single-mindedly and courageously to achieve her goal of being a writer. She wrote her first novel, *Owls Do Cry*, while staying with her mentor Frank Sargeson, and then left New Zealand, not to return for seven years. In *An Angel at My Table* (*Autobiography*, volume 2), she wrote: 'When [*Owls Do Cry*] was published, I was alarmed to find that it was believed to be autobiographical, with the characters actual members of my family, and myself the character Daphne upon whom a brain operation was performed [...] Daphne resembled me in many ways except in her frailty and absorption in fantasy to the exclusion of "reality"; I have always been strong and practical, even commonplace in my everyday life.'

She lived first in Spain, and later in England, where eventually she was assessed by specialists and liberated from the misguided diagnosis of schizophrenia. Acting on advice from her doctor ('as I was obviously suffering from the effects of my long stay in hospital in New Zealand'), she produced the novel *Faces in the Water*, an exquisitely written fictional transformation of some of the torments she had experienced and the misfortunes she had witnessed during her stays in psychiatric wards.

From this point on Janet Frame had the confidence to resist a portrayal of herself as 'crazy' simply because she wanted to live a mainly solitary life, avoiding marriage and family and a 'real' job, so that she could preserve her 'own world' – her writing. She changed her surname to Clutha (after a New Zealand river) and was issued with a new passport. She continued to write under the surname Frame and attempted to live as anonymously as possible under the pseudonym.

She wrote prolifically and later returned to New Zealand as an established author internationally acclaimed for her unique literary style in which she pushed the boundaries of the traditions she drew from and grew out of. She based herself in her home country for the rest of her life, although she travelled frequently to the United States and Britain.

In her lifetime she published eleven novels, five collections of stories, a children's book and a volume of poetry, *The Pocket Mirror* (1967). As her fame grew and readers became curious to know more about the private life behind the famous 'local girl made good', her reluctance to make more than a few rare public appearances led to a perception of her as a recluse who was unable, rather than unwilling, to jump through the publicity hoops generally expected at the release of each new volume. Her absence from the lecterns and radio waves of the nation allowed conjecture and rumour to proliferate. Exasperation at some of the myths she heard about herself, led her to attempt to 'set the record straight' in the celebrated autobiographical trilogy she wrote as she approached the age of sixty. The success of the autobiography led to even more fame, and when Jane Campion released her film adaptation, *An Angel at My Table*, Janet Frame's story became a worldwide source of inspiration far beyond her usual international literary audience. In her home country she was already affectionately regarded as a cultural icon.

Throughout her long career she received many honours at home and abroad. She was made a CBE in 1983 for services to literature, awarded an honorary doctorate of literature from Otago University in 1978, and one from Waikato University in 1992. She received New Zealand's highest civil honour in 1990 when she was made a Member of the Order of New Zealand. Janet Frame died in Dunedin in 2004.

Janet Frame's posthumous second collection *The Goose Bath* was published in New Zealand in 2006. It won the prize for best book of poetry at the annual (Montana) New Zealand Book Awards in 2007.

THE GOOSE BATH
(2006)

edited by
PAMELA GORDON,
DENIS HAROLD
& BILL MANHIRE

FOREWORD

'I've been looking through the goose bath...' Janet began saying to me after she shifted from Shannon to Palmerston North in 1989. I came to understand what she meant by this typically elliptical reference. The 'goose bath' had originally functioned as the base of a small fountain in the patio of a town house my parents bought, but the novelty of the garden ornament soon wore off. The fountain required excessive cleaning and draining so June and Wilson donated the dish to Janet's goose family for their ablutions. Janet and her new young cat Penny spent many hours out in the paddock watching the antics of Glissy and Glossy and the other geese. When Janet left the rural holding at Shannon she took the large fibreglass bowl (about the size of a child's paddling pool) back to the city with her. There, sans geese, it evolved into a convenient receptacle for Janet's burgeoning pile of poetry manuscripts built up over decades of composition and in some cases, as she would concede herself, decomposition.

'I've been looking through the goose bath' became Janet's way of describing her attempt to put together her long-awaited second volume of poetry. In an extraordinary burst of productivity over the ten years following *Living in the Maniototo* (1979), she had completed the first three volumes of her autobiography, assembled a new selection of short stories, and also written what was to be her last published novel, *The Carpathians*. Meanwhile the poetry project had been on the creative back-burner. But now she declared, publicly and privately, that it was time for her to concentrate on her poems.

Janet rarely alluded to the novel she was working on, but she was more forthcoming about her poetry. For instance, she wrote to me in 1985:

> I'm really glad you're 'into' poetry. When one goes 'into' poetry one can take so many things along – everything.... Every time I sit down to write, I write 'poetry' – I put it in inverted commas because I make no claim for its proof that I'm a 'poet' or that it is 'poetry', I only know it's fun and it leads me into interesting places. I sometimes 'fit it in' to my book, or even use it as an introductory quote...

The 'goose bath' – as we came to call her accumulation of poetry even after she had moved away from Palmerston North and discarded the actual bath – was as unruly as Janet's beloved geese had been. She struggled with the task of compiling a coherent collection. 'Some of them are rather good,' she would sometimes go on to say, or perhaps 'there's such a lot of rubbish'. As always her high standards and independent working style meant she would withhold work from the public until she was completely satisfied with it. New poems occasionally saw the light of day when Janet drew on her store to mark special occasions such as tributes to friends and colleagues, or the advent of the new millennium. Her attitude to her poems was intriguingly ambivalent. In the following excerpt from an interview recorded with Hazel de Berg in 1979, Janet appears to discount herself as a poet, yet she is simultaneously quietly confident of the value of her 'best' work:

> Poetry is my first love. I unfortunately don't feel that I've ever been able to write a real poem, but I keep trying. Perhaps that's not the way to go about it, but I tend to kill a poem. I start off and write it and then something happens and I destroy it with the wrong words. I do it every time with a poem. I see it coming. It gets to the end and I've used the wrong words and I've slipped in something that's too easy... I write what I call my best poetry, I don't publish it, but I write it just when I sit down and don't think that it is a poem.
>
> [*unpublished manuscript, Hocken Library*]

During the 1990s Janet was greatly distracted by health and other crises, as well as by the demands of her increasing fame. Much of her time and energy was also spent cooperating with her biographer Michael King. The *Life* he produced included many references to and snippets from her unpublished poems, which raised expectations in the literary community that a new collection might be in the pipeline. But by the year 2000 Janet seemed resigned to the fact that the poems would be published posthumously: when she was asked by Elizabeth Alley whether a second volume of poetry was imminent, she replied, 'I think that will have to wait until I'm dead.' The following year her fellow poet C.K. Stead commented: 'I like to think that she might be writing poems which will add another room to the house of herself she has been building for a lifetime.'

Janet's typing had become worse in her later years, especially after she developed cataracts. The deteriorating eyesight was compounded by the effects of her adventures with continually changing typewriting technology. Janet never adjusted to writing new work on the computer screen (she said the words were in the wrong place 'up in the air') although she made good recreational use of computers to email friends, compose music, play chess and simulate flight. She was an early adopter of sometimes cumbersome electronic typewriters and primitive word-processing machines that were difficult to handle, and she never fully grasped the mysteries of autocorrection and indent-setting before the next model came along and she had to learn to adapt to the new parameters all over again. She had always typed fast, not caring about typographical errors, but now the typos were more frequent.

Janet often gleefully told an anecdote about how a typo in the poem 'Christmas and Death' in the first edition of *The Pocket Mirror* made the poem take on a life of its own:

> Here is an example of a story becoming a poem – an incredibly shrinking story. A plant reduced to a single seed. Only the poem has been printed, and in the printing a mistake was made by the proof-reader who supposed I had omitted one letter of one word, and who therefore unknowingly changed the face of the poem. Where I had written *turkey*, the word became *turnkey*. The short poem has appeared in anthologies and has been read over the radio. I marvel at the fact that as it has been printed it could be described as meaningless: it is not the poem about the turkey. It is a tributary poem which, with some amusement, I trace back to the source in the story and the experience.
>
> [*undated manuscript, notes for an interview*]

We're glad she felt that way about typographical errors, because we have of course been unable to consult her on editorial decisions concerning one or two of the typing errors in poems we selected for *The Goose Bath*.

When Janet agreed in 2002 to record some of her own work for the Aotearoa New Zealand Poetry Sound Archive, she surprised everyone involved by choosing to read thirteen uncollected poems. By the time her copy of the recording arrived in her letter-box a year later, she already knew she was terminally ill and she was helping to plan her funeral. She played the CD so we could pick a suitable poem to use at the service. On hearing the poems I was astonished by their remarkable quality and the assurance of her delivery, and I exclaimed that we should publish a new volume as soon as possible, so she could receive timely accolades. 'I don't need anybody to tell me my work is good,' she said. 'Do it after I'm dead.'

She told me she had once talked to Bill Manhire about her poems and she felt he understood her poetic vision as well as her diffidence about what she saw as her failures, and that he might be able to help to select the ones that 'worked'. I met Bill not long after this, when Janet and I travelled to Gore in December 2003 for the opening of the John Money Wing at the Eastern Southland Art Gallery. With Janet's blessing, Bill and I held a first exploratory discussion about the unpublished poems. I told him that along with Denis Harold and Michael King I was going to be a 'keeper of the flame' of my aunt's literary estate, and that Janet had signalled over the years that some of her more personal writings would be available for posthumous publication. I explained that Janet had entrusted the supervision of the poetry undertaking to me and that she had suggested him as an editor she respected. Apart from that, she was too ill by then to be involved any further with the planning.

Just weeks later, in a eulogy at her public memorial service on

14 February 2004, Karl Stead exhorted Janet's estate to bring out more work from what he assumed to be a prolific stock of manuscripts. He quoted from a letter she had once written him:

> My writing is deeply involved with my life and my dreams. When I write I'm not writing to be published. Publication is always a shock and an embarrassment. I still think posthumous publication is the last form of literary decency left.

After she died I found an exercise book in which Janet had carefully noted down on page one the titles of her two most recent projects. Alongside the working title of a novel she was occupied with, she had also written the name of her elusive poetry volume: *The Goose Bath – Poems*. We have found no sign of *The Complete Book of Fear – A Novel of Incidents*. We have concluded that in her last months she must have carried out her threat to dispose of unfinished or unsatisfactory material (I had begged her to let me help her complete that work, saying she could dictate it to me, but she had said, sadly, 'It doesn't work like that.') However, as expected, an abundance of poetry – from fragmentary to fully formed – awaited inspection. Plenty of the poems were 'ready to go' and a book could have been rushed into print almost immediately, but I wanted to ensure that the work would go through a careful selection process.

I envisaged this first posthumous book of Janet's poetry not as a historic artefact, but as a book she might have been proud to publish, so I insisted that we include only those poems that were clearly viewed by Janet herself as finished pieces, and that the co-editors all agreed were worthy of her existing oeuvre. The grand academic exercise, the annotations, the unravellings, the insight for the curious into the back room of Janet Frame's creative process…these can wait. For now, our aim was to produce a living and breathing volume of the best of her uncollected poetry; one that will give pleasure to her fans and new readers alike.

We are very fortunate that Bill Manhire accepted the invitation to join me and Denis on the editorial team for *The Goose Bath*. Janet's intuition that Bill would 'know' how to deal with her poetry has been justified. His incisive, expert guidance has helped shape an elegant selection of her poems. I'm sure Janet would have been most impressed.

PAMELA GORDON

INTRODUCTION

I once sat next to Janet Frame at the dinner table. It was just after the 1994 Wellington Writers and Readers Week – a festival that had culminated in the celebration of her seventieth birthday. We started to talk, awkwardly, about poetry, and at some point I raised the subject of her own poems.

My guess, I said, was that there were lots, and that many of her readers would love to see them. Why didn't she publish them?

Well, yes, she said, there were several hundred.

'But none of them are any good. I can't keep them on a plane. They don't *end*, they fall away.'

I started talking – gabbling, really – about how the flaw, the awkward, clumsy moment, could often be what guaranteed a poem its grace as well as its authenticity.

Well, yes, perhaps, but there was a game, a posture game, she used to play with other children when she was little. It always involved fallings away, loss of poise and balance. 'You're out! Seen your eyes!' she suddenly said, in the chanting, playground voice of a small child.

She paused.

'You see, there's too much of that in my poems.' She did in fact like two of her poems very much, 'The Place' and 'Wyndham' – and 'perhaps also the one about the cabbages, and the one about the suicides. I think they work.' But that was about it.

So we talked about other things. I remember her saying how she loved the fact that everyone from Palmerston North, where she was then living, talked of 'Palmy'. The only other thing she said about poetry was that getting the rhythm right was the main thing. And she wanted her poems to be *slower*. 'Somehow I can't get that.'

If you go looking for Frame's comments on poetry, you can find a lifetime of similar moments of self-deprecation. 'I care more for poetry than prose,' she told the *Oamaru Mail* in 1962, 'but I'm not very good at it, I'm afraid.' Often the self-deprecation is accompanied by insights into what poems need and she felt hers sometimes lacked. Sending a typescript of her *Pocket Mirror* poems to George Braziller in the 1960s, she noted: 'They are technically poor, also with jiggety-jig instead of concealed rhythm...but I'm improving'. In 2000, answering Elizabeth Alley's question about why she had not published any of the poems she had written over many years, she said: 'Well I don't trust it, the poetry I write. I have a heap of poems, but none of them are real, you know? None of them are successful poems. They all trip over the old, um, rhythm and rhymes and so on, and they're not free enough.'

It's easy to see what she means about 'The Place' and 'Wyndham', both of which appeared in 1967 in her single collection of poetry, *The Pocket Mirror*. They are so simple and light and effortless – free enough, yet somehow indestructible:

The Place

The place where the floured hens
sat laying their breakfast eggs,
frying their bacon-coloured combs in the sun
is gone.

You know the place –
in the hawthorn hedge
by the wattle tree
by the railway line.

I do not remember these things
– they remember me,
not as child or woman but as their last excuse
to stay, not wholly to die.

Who could argue with the author of such a poem? And yet perhaps Janet Frame was sometimes too willing to let ideas of symmetry inflect her own voice as a poet. When she began writing seriously, an academic movement called the New Criticism ruled the English-speaking world. Poems were to be well-wrought urns – beautifully proportioned objects, entirely separate from the lives of their authors, informed by wit, elegance and paradox. W.H. Auden indicated in 1951, when introducing the first book by Frame's American contemporary Adrienne Rich, that the poems that matter are 'neatly and modestly dressed, speak quietly but do not mumble, respect their elders but are not cowed by them, and do not tell fibs'. Advice like this was general in the 1950s and 60s. To become a writer, Janet Frame would need to learn the importance of maintaining her own judgement. As she writes in her autobiography, 'Only then could I have the confidence to try to shape a novel or story or poem the way I desired and needed it to be, with both the imperfections and the felicities bearing my own signature.' Or, as she puts it in one of these poems:

I must fight and fight
with my red and yellow head
even after I am dead, to stay
my own way, my own way.

When Janet Frame was a student in Dunedin, she discovered the New Zealand journal *Landfall*, whose poems were mostly muted examples of the New Critical manner: 'obscure, scholarly, very carefully written,' she recalled in her autobiography, 'with formal stanzas and intricate rhyme and rhythm; occasionally there was a rogue free verse of half a dozen lines'. Frame's sympathies seem to be firmly with the occasional rogue free verse. We get a sense of her own preferences in a letter to Frank Sargeson commenting on C.K. Stead's first book, *Whether the Will is Free* (1964):

> I admire Karl's poems for their 'purity', and don't ask me to define purity. They remind me of clean potatoes out of the garden; the earth is washed off them (and some readers like their earth on) but their skin is a beautiful texture, and you can make necklaces only with clean potatoes. I'll have to read them again to find out if they've eyes – too many or too few.

These remarks take up the question of form and content, as if it is the roughnesses of articulation that will vouch for what is seen and said. In Frame's world, dirt is closely connected with truth and understanding – in *Owls Do Cry* the children find treasure in the town rubbish dump – and vision and insight are often to be found in what is clumsy, variegated, impure. The eyes in potatoes are those blemishes – often indicating a patch about to sprout – that we cut out before cooking. Vision, Frame seems to be saying, is rarely tidy, or polite: it interrupts the clean, pure surface. Some people cut it out.

In 'The Earthquake City' (p. 113) she talks about the 'undishevelled' journalist reporting from an earthquake-stricken city, and suggests that, by contrast, she – the poet, the citizen – can report the heartache, the tragedy, the compassion, precisely because she is dishevelled. To some extent roughness and roguishness are simply what the medium of language gives the writer. Words come with their histories of human use. The wonderful thing about them, as the playwright Dennis Potter once said, 'is that they've been in so many other people's mouths'. In a poem called 'Words', Janet Frame places language alongside arithmetic, showing that words are far more dangerous than 'clean, competent, neatly arranging numbers':

> The stain of words will soak through the thickest gloves.
> You touch them. They bite and scratch,
> your blood mixes with theirs,
> changes colour.

In another poem, 'Words Speak to Jacow Trachtenberg', the same opposition drives the argument: 'words have complexity, confusion, fluidity; / we hurt, and eat.'

In her autobiography Janet Frame describes how, living at Frank Sargeson's and 'anxious to appear working', she would spend some mornings simply typing familiar phrases – 'The quick brown fox jumps over the lazy dog', and her 'old favourite for unproductive moments', 'This is the forest primeval, the murmuring pines and the hemlock speak and in accents disconsolate answer the wail of the forest.'

Those words are from the opening lines of 'Evangeline' by Henry Wadsworth Longfellow (1807–82), a poet whose work she had once chosen for a fifth-form class prize. There is a poem that starts this way in *The Pocket Mirror*, and among Frame's papers versions of the phrase appear a number of times – working to make those unproductive moments come alive. On such occasions she was clearly typing as fast as she could: punctuation and keyboard accuracy were not important considerations, and the lines speed by. On one sheet the forest primeval quickly gives way to a memory of her father's love of 'Just a Song at Twilight', then to her sense of 'a combination of delights'; then there is a memory of Stratford hinting at the experiences in 'If I Read St John of the Cross', followed by thoughts about walking 'into the hinterland' – 'the palisade or the stars / or the mountains or the self', 'the great beyond / the back of beyond'.

And then, after some longer lines that seem to contain the first stirrings of 'The Recent Dead', she types out these words:

> This is a poem for autumn.
> And for the hinterland.
> For inklings, and the gravity star.
> How many lines to the row
> surrounded by wooden furniture
> I sit
> with music
> and tears
> perhaps I will set down
> poem after poem
> to celebrate the movement of air
> in light
> into bodies
> out of bodies
> within lives, nothing but the movement of air, the great
> exchange.

There is still some improvisation here – 'How many lines to the row' – but suddenly the words are shaping themselves into a poem.

Language is always as much subject as medium in Frame's work. And it is clear that the energies of words can lead to the surprise of meaning – 'enemy, any moan, anemone' ('The Anemone') – and to travels in unexplored territory. 'In writing,' she once told Elizabeth Alley, 'the hope is always that the imagination will come to rest in invisible places.' Maybe free association was one of the ways in which the imagination began its journey to such places. It is noticeable how many of these poems take the shape of a walk – sometimes a real walk in a real place, sometimes a walk through a subject. The impulse is always to ramble, alertly, rather than to march in step. And while Janet Frame is a writer who returns often to certain obsessions, the destination of individual poems is not always assumed at the outset. As the worksheet lines mentioned above suggest, she is frequently to be found 'walking into the hinterland'. Or, to borrow another of her phrases, she can usually be found 'far from the road labelled Scenic Drive'.

The first poem in this book – 'I take into my arms more than I can bear to hold' – points, we think, to the aim and often the activity of these poems. They make a wide embrace, gathering in whatever they can hold. There is a range of forms, from carved quatrains to the deceptively quiet perfection of

> Before I get into sleep with you
> I want to have been
> into wakefulness, too.

and from the sestina 'Tourist Season' to an anecdotal prayer like 'If I Read St John of the Cross'. But most poems seek their own direction.

There is even greater richness of content and image. Like the compass she writes of, Frame's is a sensibility which seeks to taste 'every drop of distance'. It would be hard to find a more fecund sense of the natural world in any recent writer. Birds are on the wing everywhere in these poems: crows, blackbirds, swallows, gulls, hummingbirds, bluejays, goldfinches, woodpeckers, chickadees, larks, starlings, thrushes. Likewise there are trees, plants, flowers, cats. Frame writes about weather and the change of seasons, about childhood, about the world of fairy tales and fable. She writes about oceans and cities and mountains, about mathematics, literature, poets, friends and family, music, sex. Ice and snow are here ('knives, not petals or feathers'). So is an art gallery; so is Sigmund Freud; so is the Mornington Butchery. And things and creatures are given the power of speech. In the course of *The Goose Bath* we are addressed by the Guggenheim Museum, by a brain tumour, by an anemone, by a piano, by words themselves. We even hear from Frank Sargeson's 'black tom (entire) cat'.

And just when you think you have her measure, she surprises – as in the last, audacious lines of 'Bach':

> Bach might be, say,
> a musical gossip
> writing an aural manual of fucking positions between man
> and silence
> which may or may not be called God.

God may or may not inhabit these poems, but death frequently does. 'Poetry has not room for timidity of tread,' Frame writes in 'Some of My Friends Are Excellent Poets', and one of her least timid qualities is her willingness to look hard at what damages us most: our own extinction. She wrote a number of quite distinct poems titled 'The Dead' during her life – one appeared in *The Pocket Mirror*, another in *Landfall* (Vol 11, p. 148, 1957); another is in this book. In *The Goose Bath* words to do with death or the grave easily outnumber the pages of the collection itself. As she notes in one poem, 'the principal thing seen and dreamed is Death'.

There might have been many ways of shaping this book. The most obvious would have been to print the poems in order of composition. But that would have meant many years of scholarly sifting, of checking manuscript archives, trying to understand about different typewriters and word-processors, as well as different kinds of typing paper. It would also have involved developing more than a provisional understanding of the relationships between different drafts and recensions of individual poems, many of which exist in several apparently final versions. And in such cases, which version would we have chosen? The one we thought most poetically pleasing, or the one we thought most recent? At a very simple level, what would we have done with 'A Specimen in the Maudsley Brain Museum'? That poem was published in the autobiography with the date 1955 in its text, but there is a typescript where the author has crossed out 1955 by hand, replaced it with 1985, then crossed that out in favour of 1975. In fact, we have almost always preferred what we took to be the most recent version of a poem. But a scholarly account of the available material might have seen a dozen years pass before Janet Frame's unpublished poems became available.

We thought of other ways of arranging these poems, too, but in the end settled on a shape that follows the course of a human life – from childhood to ageing and retrospect and death – and that, in its seven sections, often overlaps with the phases of Janet Frame's own life. Thus we have grouped together poems about her years in London and Europe. Likewise poems about her many trips to the United States are gathered in a single section. In a very loose and inexact way this collection gives some sense of what a further volume of autobiography might have looked like: the crowded world of relationships and travel; the moments of mischief and joy; the energy and courage of the clear-sighted, confident woman whom Michael King so richly portrayed in *Wrestling with the Angel*.

We are proud of *The Goose Bath*, and pleased with the shape we have given it. We admire Janet Frame as a writer even more than we did before we began this work. But we also acknowledge that this is not the book she would have made.

BILL MANHIRE

THE GOOSE BATH

I Take into My Arms More Than I Can Bear to Hold

I take into my arms more than I can bear to hold
I am toppled by the world
a creation of ladders, pianos, stairs cut into the rock
a devouring world of teeth where even the common snail
eats the heart out of a forest
as you and I do, who are human, at night

yet still I take into my arms more than I can bear to hold

1

A Dream

I dreamed there was a stone wall,
and a sun, shaped like Humpty Dumpty,
round and fat, sitting there;
but no warmth came from the sun.
He smiled, opening a cold yellow mouth.
Ha Ha, he said. I am in the centre of things
but I shall not keep you warm for ever.

Just then a black cat with its face burned
walked slowly and delicately along the wall.
The sun lashed at it
with a stick made of ice and covered with snow.
– Be off, he said sharply.

I woke then, and it was morning,
with a bird-note falling down and down
like a long long sigh of surprise.

Goldfinch

When I was small and sick
my father brought in a goldfinch
to fly around the room.
He was bringing in the sun.

It panicked
In wanting Out
beat its forehead
upon the heavenly window.

The Tooks and the Gaves
are spilling blood
The Gives and the Takes
are full of love.

My goldfinch
bones like wires growing
yellow paper flowers
threaded light like a bead in his eye

his beak hissing
for the fresh air
– Lift the roof O my child
and trust the sky.

Story

Blood fell upon the snow
in the first fairytale I knew.
The childless Queen, I remember,
pricked her finger
and wished to harbour within
her body pink flesh and fair skin,
and thus without difficulty
unmatched physiologically
a princess was born
Hello little Snow-White!

Later when such tales were dim
when symbols were shattered
and Freud mattered
more than Grimm
red fell upon white
when Lily and Ted
in the hotel bed
bloodied the sheet.
Hello little Rose-Red!

The tale is sad.
Both Snow White and Rose Red
were beaten
and eaten.

Worms

There was a time, weeks, months of prosperity.
Lawns were green, the sky was blue,
the wild sweet peas were in pink bud along the railway cuttings.
My father played golf on Sundays
until we unravelled the golf balls to locate the bounce.
My newest sister crawled around in her box
in the sun near the cowbyre.

And I had worms.

I saw them!
I looked down after I had finished one day and I saw them,
little white things wriggling in it.

– Worms, my mother said in a horrified voice. – Worms!
– The child's got worms!
My father exclaimed, looking fiercely at me,
– Worms? Worms!

I went outside in the sun.
I sat among the daisies and the dandelions in the grass,
all by myself, because I had worms.

Child

When I was a child I wore a fine tartan coat
that my grandmother, woman of might,
magnificent launcher of love and old clothes, had set afloat
on a heaving relative sea
of aunt and cousin and big enfolding wave of mother
down to small wave of me.

Oh happily I stood that day in the school playground
near the damp stone wall
and the perilous nine o'clock wind
grabbed at my coat-sleeve, waving it in a bright wand
of yellow and green and blue
– all colours, and the other children loved me
and the little girls pleaded to lend
their skipping-rope and the boys their football.

But the spell soon broke in my hand.
Love and sleeve together fell.
The wind blew
more perilous when the world found
my tartan coat was not even *new*.

A Simple Memory of a Poet, a Memory Shuffled Face Upward

Wearing my golden secondhand clothes I think of Mary Ellen Blair who was
                                                          partially blind
sitting among the kowhai blossoms.
She wore dark glasses like eclipses of the moon
on the verandah at Tulliallan.

Her poems were privately collected on slippery paper that, having no printhold,
allowed the words to slide downhill into the ravine
beneath the eclipsed moon.
She wrote of kowhai blossoms, old gold, and was labelled that kind of poet,
which she was! Kowhai blossoms, roses, birds, the sky,
the sea and the people of her immediate family.
Limitless themes in a limiting limited time
when so many words lay inaccessible, lost in the ravine
beneath the eclipsed moon.

I remember my mother sighing used to say,
Mary Ellen Blair the poetess, her lovely poems. She is partially blind.
She lives at Tulliallan.

My mother had never been privately printed.
Yet perhaps one day her words would grow on the
creviced public pages; salt thorn bushes
covered with minute blue flowers.

It was a hope she had, my public mother standing at convenient corners
                              like a neighbourhood dairy or filling station,
while Mary Ellen Blair on the verandah of Tulliallan
in her fullpage photograph
sat proudly in the frontispiece as by a fireside
of kowhai blossom
wearing her eclipses of the moon.

The Child

A mountain of care pressed upon the child. He could never remove it.
His world was neat. He had everything.
Storms came out of his father, silences were born in his mother,
and stayed, spread like a patch of disease or the places in the earth where
the locusts came.

He wondered would the locusts eat the city and its vegetation and people?
Were the buildings vegetation?
The buildings were tall like coconut palms and at night
the thousands of windows burned with light
as if the neat woodpecker holes in the coconut palms
were made into windows, as if the insects had spoken –

Let's be people with windows and lights
let's look out at night upon the high world of sky.
Or had the people said, Let's be insects?
Then, the woodpecker might be waiting to fly into the city,
to breakfast upon the people.

The child had everything. I am afraid of nothing, he said.
He puckered his tiny face with pain
he stared out of his eyes like a tiny animal staring fearfully from its burrow
at the weather in the sky, woodpecker-high.

Tap-tap. Knock-knock knock. Tap tap tap. Knock.
He lay still, shivering. He had seen the insects look out.
Had the woodpecker come for his supper?
He screamed. A light snapped on. 'I had a bad dream.'
He was not afraid. His face puckered into old age.
He had everything, everything.
The woodpecker was waiting for him and would wait for ever.

For Paul on His Birthday

We shared a childhood. We were the railway children
playing quiet games while our father slept through the day.
Our world was a hush-hush world. We both found a wand,
pencil and paper, to enchant our silence.
You remember?

How strange, waking in the night, with eyes burning, limbs asleep, voices agrizzle.
Our house was candle-lit and lamplit.
Our father roved the ceiling with his arm while he breakfasted.
My tired mother, her long red hair unpinned, lit the fire,
pulled out the damper, and the flames roared and the kitchen was warm.
You watched your sister moving like a princess trapped in a maze.
Reste tranquille, si soudain
l'Ange à ta table se décide.
In your house and mine there were screams in the night:
your mother, my brother.
You and I grew up remembering,
holding fast to our quiet pencils
(which Freud, in his envy, might have given another name)
moving out of the golden desert land. Matagouri? Sage-brush?
Cactus, rattlesnake, mountain lion. Frowning rock foreheads.
(Giants overcome by butterflies.)

Hush, our fathers are sleeping.
The Great Train Robbery is over; also,
our first-class free tickets are no longer valid.
It is you, now, who make the meals of enchantment.
Reste tranquille, si soudain
l'Ange à ta table se décide,
on this, your birthday.

The Happy Prince

In the children's record of the Happy Prince,
before each gold flake is peeled from the Prince's body,
the voice orders, Turn the Page, Turn the Page,
supposing that children do not know when to turn,
and may live at one line for many years,
sliding and bouncing boisterously along the words,
breaking the closed letters for a warm place to sleep.
Turn the Page, Turn the Page.

By the time the Happy Prince has lost his eyes,
and his melted heart is given to the poor,
and his body taken from the market-place and burned,
there is no need to order, Turn the Page,
for the children have grown up, and know when to turn,
and knowing when, will never again know where.

I Visited

I visited
the angels and stars and stones;
also, adjectival poets, preferably original.
There was an air of restlessness
an inability to subside, a state of being at attention,
at worst, at war with the immediately beating heart and breathing lung.
I looked then in the word-chambers, the packed warehouses by the sea,
the decently kept but always decaying places where nouns and their
representative images lay together on high shelves
among abbreviations and longlost quotations. I listened.
Water lapped at the crumbling walls; it was a place
for murder, piracy; salt hunger seeped between the shelves;
it was time to write. Now or never. The now unbearable,
the never a complete denial of memory:
I was not, I never have been.

A Room

It had walls like these walls
only shit-stained, and light
like this room only caged and
the door, inside, was without a handle.

And all day I heard the children
calling out of their white waxen mouths
looking out of their tar-black eyes that shone
like dream highways, thruways, freeways
beaten down by journeying silence.

They played with bloodstained toys. Two barked
like dogs. They were dressed in butchers' smocks
and their feet were swollen like castles;
and there was always the child, aged three,
locked in and whispered about because
his head was an oak-leaf and his mouth was absent.

How did he live so long without spitting
at the stone that weighed down on him?
He might easily, so simply, have fallen like rain
upon himself and been washed away
to sleep in earth with armchair spiders and yellow teardrop flowers.

Hilda

Hilda had a squinted heart
stared with uncombed locks of vision
upon a fire that none put out,
that no one saw. It was the sun,

the raw left-over from creation,
the ragged spare half-yard of light
by gypsy of amnesia sewn
to canvas pitched in paddock of night.

So they gave her glasses with deceiving
lens to try to make her mind
surrender the insane believing
that world is fire and men are blind.

So they tore and stamped and poured fond
average floods of sense – like normal
firemen treating a flaring mind
who quench their private view of hell.

Now Hilda lives as sensibly
as any woman, and the sun's
Antarctica as far as she
is burned by it or strange visions.

But the retired firemen, their wives and sons
still grind their bones in bedroom dark
to try to flint the quenched visions
of Hilda with her squinted heart.

Hospital Dance

Shake shake hazel tree
grown from these tears of pity
to twig catkin husk enfolding
this night's fruit, their treasure.

Shake love which they most need
the festive fabric spread
to cover fear, unshape
their intolerable privacy.

Shake words to fit
the world's blind edict
of sense that their mouths' talk
tonight untongue all dread.

More than one prince and princess
will twirl weave thread
a sense of speech and love
through the night's maze of dance
beneath the unreal dream-blaze
of no chandelier's brilliance.

The old king, the father,
bald, benevolent, his heart
overlapping, fretting like sea
upon the lost land
of his last sane wish
chooses, encloses his queen's hand.

I Do Not Want to Listen

I do not want to listen
I refuse to listen
to the geometric noises
of black and white.

My big colourful mouth
has enough to eat thank you
without tasting
a plain triangle or two.

Yes, I know rain-
drops are as heavy
and colourless as stones
and fall tropically

rain-bashing what
scurries
without obvious form
and certainly without hope

to the defining
shelter of a microscope.
And I've heard
of stick insects and figures

and striped beds
in the sky and rows
of disembodied black
and white flowers yet

poor as rainbows are
against the pressure
and purity
of no-colour

I must fight and fight
with my red and yellow head
even after I am dead, to stay
my own way, my own way.

I'm Invisible

I'm invisible.
I've always been invisible
like poverty in a rich country,
like the rich in the secretive rooms of their many-roomed houses,
like fleas, like lice, like growth beneath the earth,
worlds beyond the sky, the wind, time, ideas –
the catalogue of invisibility is endless,
and, they say, does not make good poetry.

Like decisions.
Like elsewhere.
Like institutions far from the road labelled Scenic Drive.

No more similes. I'm invisible.
In a people-world of binocular vision I'm in the majority after all
as you and I walk with our tiny crescent moon of sight in our personal darkness
through a world where decisions of being and not-being
are controlled by light
helped by tears and the sleep of inattention or death.

I'm invisible.
The lovers reach through my life to touch each other,
the rain falling through me courses like blood upon the earth.
I am carried in no one's head as knowledge.
I give freedom to the dancers,
to the speaking of truth.
It is this way. There's no one here to eavesdrop or observe,

and then I learn more than I am entitled to know.

The Tom Cat Which Sargeson Refused to Have Neutered

Sargeson's black tom (entire) cat
out all night
sleeping late
stretched on the mat,
leaves a note,

Call me at three or four.
I want to wash and polish my fur
with a bit of cat spit, have a bite to eat,
before I take a preliminary prowl to haunts of court
to put as it were my card out.

I think I suit this orgy of meet and mate.
Though I'm neither grate nor ingrate
I think I thank the eternal Cat for it.
So, Frank,
call me at three from my sleeping-place on the mat.
Yours,
the black tom (entire) cat.

To FS Who Shaved His Beard

Grow back your beard, your overflowing white hedge
set as barrier between your shack of words and time
the never-never salesman who tries to kiss awake from pillow
of bracken on mud floor the played-out and paid-for word,
who tries to trick with talk of cosier bungalow,
cantilever terrace, clearer death-view of Rangitoto.

Renew the oath made in summer to your unshaven self
to wave defiantly your home-made flag if time comes too close,
and remember when you light your lamp in the hovel of word-care
to blanket the sleeping word with your white beard. You may not sleep.
Though night be sucked in by cicada you guard your starved shack
yet nearer to castle if seen through prism of this white hedge,
flax, treefern, and flash of kingfisher.

2

Choosing Postcards

Now I've travelled to the forbidden foreign land
where the whole world lives, masquerading as 'the other half '.
(Boundaries, discreetly drawn, even if
they cut across home, make reason for grand
scientific discoveries.)
                               Now my desperately pivoting mind
slows down. It is time for me to choose
a significant postcard from the many shopworn human views
displayed – (Am I perhaps afraid of what I shall find?)

Here's the technicolour suicide that's inclined
to seem unreal, so many are sent from abroad,
they're garish in this real light... By the way, did you see
this new enlarged photo of me?
(I stress the relaxed, the intimate attitude.)

In the dingy shop I'm crying. I believe
I don't know what to choose or what to believe.

A Visitor to Cornwall

Hands praying for souvenirs and ice-cream,
hungry pantechnicon eyes hauling London goods and chattels
to furnish the bare sea-sprayed shop windows,
ecstatic voices in unquestioning agreement with the sea's point of view.
No! I said, I'll never live here in July and August,
I'll stay in the quiet season, I'm a cut above the ordinary tourist –
There'll be no counting of wounds or comparative measurement of blood,
but I'm not like the others, I'm different,
I'm at home here, accepted as a native of the place. (Dreams
thus flatteringly make us a cut above ourselves.)

All right. I'm a stranger. I send postcards and curios,
write letters beginning –I met a colourful
personality, an old identity who could speak the language
as it flourished before the words sickened died and were buried
in the churchyard on the hill where the tombstones rear sharp and white
like rows of crippled seagulls' wings guarding the graves, I'm having
a wonderful time, I've settled in,
the way of life is picturesque,

the way of death more so;
the streets murmur with the muffled hooves of the spring tide,
the green-painted shop-doors swing like stable-doors; the place
is completely unspoiled, there's a church
in a plain grey dress of stone
with dark ivy necklace.
The houses face the sea, huddle shoulder to shoulder above the harbour,
the seagulls drift and fall –
All right, I'm a stranger!
                    My family tree
cannot be traced to the roots of the first sea-abused thorn
growing out of these cliffs to face life-long
bewitchment by sunlight and storm.
I've no graves to visit to feed flowers
like pink pills to pale memories, I've no direction,
How can I get to? If I take this path where will I arrive at?
The fingers of the unfamiliar signposts accuse me.
I'm a stranger. I don't belong here.

I'll win yet, given time and cunning.
I'll pattern my past experience in a neat web to trap
an acceptance that is more than Christian names, weather greetings,
a willingness to keep newly-baked bread for me, beyond the promised hour.
For I *know* the sea, I've lived by it all my life,
I can pick holes in its arguments as big as caves or bomb-craters,
I know the sea by heart, its tricks, its pretence,
I've never agreed with its opinions
obsessively intoned as it labours the meaning
at the dark lectern
in unfeeling literal translation
cribbed from the moon's profit on the earth's professional leaning.

All right. I'm a stranger. But I'll not gape at the sea,
or marvel at the gulls and their gabbling auction
or the fanciful names painted on the hulls
of the fishing-boats.
I'll not shout extravagantly from the top of Polkirt Hill,
A wonderful view! A wonderful view!
Such remarks are only in fashion among visitors to Outer Space.
Instead, I'll admire and love silently, close to the source,
like a native. When my home-sick blood flows
I'm a cut above the ordinary tourist, a cut or festered gash.
I belong with the gulls and the smugglers' ghosts, my roots are among
white clay, and blackthorn lardered with salt high on the cliff-shelf
– sea-stored, sea-raided, the Atlantic recipe.
(The Pacific is too many thousand miles away.)

All right. I'm a stranger. I've still no direction.
I can't even come home to myself.
I weave a neat web, yet I'm no needlewoman
to put stitches in
my own skin.

The Unhappy Island

It is an unhappy island. Rain falling
perpetually has soaked the earth, its grasses,
the leaves of the trees; and any people living here walk no more
not being able to bear the sodden burden of their flesh
that grows moss, green moss turning gold in autumn, in spring
blossoming with white flowers minute as nerve-endings.
Here there is no speech of people. Their voices
are filled wells, pools, stagnant ponds,
their eyes instruments of light used to distort the image.
They cannot sleep or dream. All sound
is rain falling for ever, the world a mould
an overgrowing moss in the midst, strangely, of a clear ocean.
A real island, a rumoured continent; and here no salt,
no salt. The rain, the creeks, the lakes have no traces of tears.
Nobody ever cried here, my darling!

The Icicles

Every morning I congratulate
the icicles on their severity.
I think they have courage, backbone,
their hard hearts will never give way.

Then around ten or half past,
hearing the steady falling of drops of water
I look up at the eaves. I see
the enactment of the same old winter story
– the icicles weeping away their inborn tears,
and, if they only knew it, their identity.

Tenant

The man living here before me
was a shady character, rather lonely,
but at home in his room
– in and out like a worm in a ripe apple.

He was dirty, he spilled
slops at the door, and killed the hollyhocks.
He sat up late at night reading
and stained the best wallpaper with hair-oil.

No, he didn't bath. He never turned the radio up loud.
He came from somewhere the back of beyond
where they sit under lemon trees, and ask
riddles of giant vermilion cattle with white faces.

One thing in his life – there was a tortoise.
Like a crude brooch worn across his heart, it sat
brown and flat and quiet – except
it sparkled when he spoke to it.

The Stones

The day is grey.
The sun has only sixpence worth of shine,
and the stones breed.
I did not say *bleed*, though they are hurt
day and night by shoes and wheels
and speared with umbrella-sticks
and the white arrows of the few acknowledged blind.
These make no wound.
Yet the pink reflection in the sky at night is curiously
like the reflection of diluted blood.
What part of the city is it that bleeds
secretly, so that it shows in the night sky?

Is it the stones? They breed,
create their problems of possession, crowd out the human race;
they feed on centuries, not on other stones.
They are also self-consuming, they breed and walk the city
stone after stone rolling soundlessly

47

silently rioting in the square,
or signing the deed of grass that is its green blood
spurting pallid and diseased at the stones' overturning.

The day is grey.
Love sprung from, in treaty with, loveliness
has bred, consumed itself, filled the square with riot
of silence and time
then overturned
as stone, as plate and slate of marvel
where men are served and swallowed, written and learned,
when skimmed on the dark water stone is the shadow of a cathedral.

The Underground

It is not monster or desert track yet it seems so
with the dark roaring
and the hot wind
and the hand of the clock uncovering from the sand
the daily pyramid, the stone faces remote in burial.

'Take the escalator,' they say, who live their own lives,
who make love, and fight against the shade the sun provides;
but the escalator takes them, and they are lived,
and their love makes them, and their shadow
fights to measure their flesh and wear their fine clothes.

So they go down past the colonisation of stars,
past the spying of snowfall
on a dry planet disciplined with fire,
to the future, to yesterday's caves
now embroidered with fruit, soothing syrup, breakfast wheat.

And the same tribe paddles the flat world
till it turns round again with many seas;
they suffer flood, famine, more than two wars,
and being in the dark and without speech, whimper, and hit sticks against
                                                                          the trees,
then scratch the sun, a clean circle, on the cave wall.

A Specimen in the Maudsley Brain Museum

Parker's tumour, nineteen fifty-five!
You could not see it through his balding head
or in his clouded face, or hear it speaking
in his wild cries, though it fanged forth speech
in snakely blossoming unreason.
                         He spent his last years hiding
under a cliff of circular reptiles and raging sunlight till one day
a landslide of weightless rock fell and Parker died.

His cremation was at Golders Green, a service held
in the private chapel, solemnly his virtues extolled
(the jetsam of vice as yet concealed by the full tide of grief).
His widow rented a niche for his ashes in the church wall,
and gave the wreath-money for Tumour Research.
But few at the ceremony ever dreamed they burned
and buried less of Parker than it seemed.

Another lantern-slide. Another joke. Nightfall.
The room empties. Layers of cold cling to the varnished
furniture. Once more the bottled and labelled thing is set aside
on the cluttered desk among files and case-histories.
Like an unblessed mariner mistaking vanity for compulsion
it tells how Parker died: With my double tongue I spat
at God. In formalin my prestige grows fat. I survive
as Parker's Tumour, nineteen fifty-five.

The Servant

The room has double doors. Unobtrusively entering, the servant takes his place,
                                        waiting to be summoned
by signals he has learned long ago to understand and respond to.
His face is in darkness. A towel
draped over his arm will clean away unsightly stains of flesh and blood
spilled in the performance of his duties.
Beside him, also in darkness, is the store of provisions
from which he is given the responsibility of choosing those which, to him,
                                        seem appropriate.

How polite he is with every offering!
He will put forward two or three choices, speaking softly, formally
– Do you care for this? For this?

Yet he has no air of a salesman forcing his goods upon an unwilling buyer.
He remains the servant always.
He shows no dismay or frustration if what he offers is rejected.
Nor does he question the source, unknown to him, of his offerings.
He knows only that when he arrives to begin work the supply is there.
– Would you care for? Would you rather?
Self-effacing, servant language.
He makes no recommendations, indulges in no reminiscences.
He has no life beyond this room.
Leaving the room he disintegrates, transformed to nothingness,
the flesh and blood stained towel is pulped to a vague substance, a vanishing
                              shadow, faintly red like a wound-mark.

You may say that perfect servants and waiters are a vanished race
that no human being must ever serve another, that the
appearance and dress I describe are obstinately old fashioned, unoriginal,
that a selection of supplies would be made more skillfully by machine.
– Why? You ask. – Why clothe what waits upon you in such cumbersome
ridiculous human manners and dress?

I will tell you why.
Sometimes at the end of day
when torn words, phrases, the flesh and blood of mutilated sentences
lie heaped upon the floor of this room,
the perfect servant, this provider of images and the dreams that inspire them,
after he has wiped clean the floor and the walls and the desk
and himself, and the exposed places of my own skin,
will approach me and, suddenly, shrunk to the size of a child-waif, will cry
– I do not want to become nothing!
Let me stay, let me stay all night in this room, in the warm!

And then it is I who fetch and carry and offer, choose dreams and their images
while the perfect servant, myself, sleeps dreamlessly,
smiling as no machine ever smiled
with the promised renewal, pleasure and toil of tomorrow.

The Simple Shepherds

But the simple shepherds never were that
and no one ever imagined they were
though most could not read or write
or count beyond ten or twenty sheep – one sheep to each finger and toe.
The arithmetical aids in the field, however, were many:
after the body, grassheads, rocks, stones
broken twigs laid in rows of ten and twenty
enough to check the day's tally of living and dead sheep and shorn fleeces.

The simple shepherd – let us call him that –
had no need to write.
What is the mind like that is not crisscrossed, webbed, patterned
with wire words secure in their alphabets?
It must be like a field of new snow
shadowed by unique shapes
the spontaneous swiftly-dissolving impression of ideas
as if a whole forest melted
in the few moments of the simple shepherd's respiration.
Or like a view of the sky in a world without vegetation or architecture;
standing in a place exposed to winds raging from the farthest corners of thought
                                                                                    and dream;
knowing an inner stereoscopic vision
unhindered by the boundaries of the binocular word.

If I did not feel fairly accustomed to my literate time
and if I did not often need to shelter in a word from the dream's hazard
I might envy the simple shepherd.

Nails as a Rose

Nails as a rose,
nails with tiny heads blunted of reason
hammered by iron held by a hand
at the end of an arm at the end of a brain
at the end of a nail at the end of a thorn;
coffin nails marching down down
two inch three inch
roofing nails with hats on battered sombreros
slender nails young and hard shining silver
nails gathered together persuaded as people are persuaded

into groups, clouted from left to right;
who has built our house of roses,
who has sheltered us with roses
who has hanged crucified buried us with roses
roses hammered by iron held by a hand
at the end of an arm at the end of a brain
at the end of a nail at the end of a thorn?
Roses, nails,
roses have cradled us fed us
hanged crucified buried us
roses with blunt heads that have no thorns
roses suffering their own thorns
that they might cradle feed us
hang crucify bury us
bloodless roses
faint flush of pink only in their heart
blood-hint sun-hint;
it is nothing, no we are not wounded; leave it;
it will heal soon;
we are not wounded by
a strange poisonous thorn
but by one
that belongs to us, grows from us,
its point in our heart and centre.

A Field of Wheat

Wheat is the almost perfect brotherhood,
perhaps because it does not speak
or because it agrees to move the same way when the wind blows,
but under pressure, standing room only.
It listens, ripens. There's no law against
such a crowd, upright, on its best behaviour.
– What's on? say slept-in poppies, toast-brown morning hares,
new blind mice, toads bleeding at the mouth
in the middle of the road, like wounded lava.
– What's the dignified, discreet assembly?
Off with their heads, we'll see what they're hiding,
we'll find out the mystery
of such close brotherhood that shares the same shadow
of the clouds, which inclines to the same view,
sleeps standing up, listening, listening.

The reapers come, the deed is done, the secret is out.
The wheat is hiding nothing but its own roots.
Shame at its origins?

Blackbird Hanging Out Your Bait

Blackbird hanging out your bait
for the spring fish to take
that's swimming green and yellow
deep down where the dead lie like pirates
comfortably patched over one eye –
this poem on a city
heath where
the smoke is homeless and won't go home
is truth only
in a lilac tree outside a window
of the place I most know where I do not live now,
where they say (between blackbirds)
Make ready the spare room, frost has come to stay.
He works nightshift and overtime and hangs around all day
under mosses, birch trees.

Down in the city Spring has arrived
perennial as a sale of railway lost property,
selected, sunlit, as a tier of Spanish oranges,
green, glassy, go-ahead as a traffic light.
Women crowd the fashion stores; men
gaze dreaming in windows that display
welding materials and streamlined
electric precision tools.
      Blackbirds may sing
on the shore, of the season that got away;
the pigeons, matronly sirens, dive for their prey;
Can't you hear them gurgling in the smoky bath?

Norfolk Evening

In the age-old evening
women with work-ridden faces like leather saddles,
hair sleek, black as waxed thread, hands like forked carrots, feet like nobbled
                                                potatoes growing bigger and bigger
in the misfit world, weed their plots against the wilderness of death or hoping
for flowers and fat pulses, shovel dung in.

North Sea gas,
moon-landing, a murder on the Common, hearts roasting evenly behind the
                                                glass panel,
a husband's belly shingle-studded, star-itching,
scratch a scab of dust, uncover
the rich earth, the rain-filled earth that will cover,
recover important promises kept.

The Church door
is shut with grass, nettles, splashed with starling-shit;
the grey flint bones shine best in winter sun;
the few stay-at-home words last a life-time –
all flesh is flint, nettles, starling-shit (the door never opens)
blue swallows inking the telegraph wires, grass.

Slow country people
yours and mine, he and she eating each other as animal eats vegetable,
the North Sea wind's the skin of their bodies, the red bouncing sun
each born head marigold-sprouting in the garden,
their age-old plot the speechless evening arriving
with its unlucky stroke of dark.

3

The Advice of Light

Cloud-curious
embalmed among the planets
lavishly clothed with stars
man is certainly
a dead flag
and he has no country
and he wears the borrowed scars of the moon.

The pinpoint of space is on Earth
brushed by a General's breast
thumbprinted with war and wherever
fingers travel
to all the spyholes of the body.

Nothing can touch me, says Light
intimate with my eye.
And I believe it,
I must believe it.
I call on light to make a universal noise
of triumph in itself
to make us listen and say
Here at last is the welcome advice of light.

Blame the Tokarahis

Blame the Tokarahis
or that raw wind coming past the Freezing Works from Pukeuri
or the Kakanuis topped with snow. Sunny Oamaru
in past Novembers was never bleak or cold,
never like this.

Never like this. The refrain stays and hurts; words that even stones
who should know refuse to speak; but people may
who dare not call home their dreams of immutability
from their petrified distant array.
They make fine statues in the sun
The unchanging sun is their ally.

Who spoke of war?
Home-coming is dangerous as ever.
I want my death to stay in the distant paddocks shining in the sun
all day till night.
I'll sit by this pine tree remembering
the purple ice-plant, the creeper
(its juice cures the warts of children).
Still the shamrock stems grow to be bitten and sucked,
the periwinkle flower yields honey.

Sweet Corn

Licking, lapping the low trough of sky,
sweating summer like a collie's green tongue,
the season's sweet corn has risen in orderly
rows from foul disorder of my spirit's dung.

It was here that I buried my past words, verse
bred with Freud and other heroes upon innersprung
double bed of libraries, lupins and gorse,
under fairydown candlewick aircell coverlet of dreaming.

The sweet corn knows nothing of this, disdains
me. The rows of whip-thin leaves grow
slantwise to share fairly the November rains
prevailing winds and sun, and give no

sign that I helped prepare their ripe cages
filled, soundlessly, with marbles of gold grain
like fire-locked years imprisoned within ages,
cells of time and pride no man may open.

The Crocodile

Your cluster of yellow teeth
topples like Stonehenge.
Have you swallowed morning sunlight,
many Druids?

Like a young poet
you have frog's eyes,
horny growths on your tongue,
and you open your mouth to advertise
widely, tirelessly.

Or, crocodile, you die.
A spear thrown
where your armour is thin;
the beautiful river drained away
leaving a handsome wallet, vanity-case,
a pair of new shoes to keep our feet warm and dry,
to walk in
over the stones, the stones of your silence.

The Leech

It is good to get back
out of every medical treatise and book
into the pure leech-track.

Out of bottles and jars on shelves
into still-raging insect wars
getting a spyhole to or at least hearing about the stars.

Catching up on history – our ancestors
and the Leech-Gatherer now long dead
the old man who propped up the world.
Applied by a poet to a feverish poem
our multi-great grandfather
found himself
unexpectedly sucking the *poet's* blood.

Ah! Yet something is lost! To be
in your own being a remedy,
a pet vampire, famously blood-hungry.

No doubt about it: the old leech days are gone.
We must feel our thirst desperately to want to press on
trying to get blood out of the sick stone.

And the Sound of the Cellos

And the sound of the cellos.
And the sound of the cellos was heard in all the land.
And the faces of the dead were covered with white cloth, with lawn,
as of lawn handkerchiefs of olden times,
and the olden times came home to the dead, as they do, for the olden times
lie forever in wait.

Wrong Number

It is not the right time to telephone me.
I have been emptying ashes
from two fires,
getting rid of the old bodies of embers
with traces in my hair and eyes
stinging and
flames freshly bleeding where I struck the hot coals
meaning only to bring about
a deathbed
revival as I promised, setting my speech
to match the fires frail whispering,
I must be
cruel (surely you have heard it!) to be kind.
But I am tired and it is not
the right time
to telephone me and ask in a strange voice
Hello is that the Mornington
Butchery.

I Met a Man

I met a man who wore a winter suit.
He played the flute.

I met a man who sang carols by a bonfire.
He was a liar.

I met a man who dug his grave too early.
His hair was curly.

The moral is, the strangest people go
about the earth. Don't you think so?

I met myself moralising
eating a cake with white icing.

Fleas Are Fleas

Fleas are fleas
because they do as they please,
they hop, do not sneeze,
and suck blood
from places where it is rude
for a flea
to be.

The Weapon

Now it is people. Meeting.
How all our arrows of liking, disliking
strike the same target.
– Ourselves, who feel the pain and pleasure
but do not yet show it.
It is a game we play
to pierce all the surfaces with love.

Saintly, then, we turn
to embrace.
The tagged arrows read
An end to loss.
And in fine print
(who reads fine print?)
Poison. Do not use.

Love Poem

Your being stone-blind is all I need
to banish in the black season what will shine;
I mean day, the always invading sun –
glittering again rainbow and manifold
unbattening the hatch of dark above the nude
cave of night, hungrily flooding in
with heave of colour, myriad waves of pain,
confounding darkness with prismatic misdeed.

All I need is your being stone-blind,
your power to shudder daylight back and back,
encased in globe of dark to face first dark,
and then dead colour, and knowing him dead, bind
his body and wipe his wound clean, your hand
dipped in light from some maintained daybreak
of heart from where no black season of self may take
stored sun, nor may even being dead or stone-blind.

A Journey

Yes. We will sleep together.
We will mix juices
to put out the fire,
arrive at the Poles
from the Equator
without a scar,
with only a handful
of unidentified
ashes.

Before I Get into Sleep with You

Before I get into sleep with you
I want to have been
into wakefulness, too.

4

Drought in Another Country

At home
news is in the ruin of cattle, sheep, crops,
the premature dying of sight from the TV's eye;
out of town, the tapping of iron tanks to hear
the panic echo of the last few drops of rainwater
faintly hiccupping against the dimpled iron.

It is the land lying sick, suntouched, disfigured with sores
in a weatherpose that will not turn.
At home,
I have heard that, officially,
drought is three weeks without rain.

Here, in another country
renowned for technological midwifery
where ice is born in the icebox,
milk in a sealed carton,
water from the head of a shining faucet,
drought is a slowly creeping sickness.
'We could feel the effect the winter following next summer.'

Now, the wind blowing from the desert
eats the ivy that knits a shawl of chain stitch
to cover the crumbling earth.
Even the pampered houseplant,
the pink and crimson horse's ear,
dies out of sympathy,
asserting its pathetic fallacy
here, in Berkeley.

Suddenly it is a world of animal, bird, reptile pilgrimage.
The diamond-backed rattlers have come out of the hills,
the grey deer run through the garden,
the cedar waxwings have left the High Sierras.
Thirsty as pilgrims
they come to drink
from the miraculous garden hose,
the green plastic fountain
that blossoms its own life-giving
Sears (hardware) rose.

The Guggenheim Museum, New York

To view the public hangings
a pastime they have long been accustomed to
the people blaze their cultural trail downward inside me
demanding, How do you pronounce *Klee*?
Klee? Fire-clay? Or Klee, the pattern of a bird's cry
above grey and white water solidified in oil
(the news has not yet reached the submerged mammals
who must come to the surface to breathe
or the mermaids with nowhere now to enact their betrayal).

Water is sliding, spilling over thin tongues of glass
arranged on my separate floors in *tiers* as if each tongue were
an apartment tasting and spit-raining people, returning them
to the heart of the fountain.
                              What marvels
are contained in my shell, enough to invite
the sun to swoop down without charity
to take my intestines my flesh my bones my tourist parasites
this loving perplexed ineradicable infection
for choicest meat.
                    Swoop, sun and sky and blackbird
upon my solid unfearful pearl! It is you
will break *your* wings and light against my shell!

An Exhibit in the Pre-Columbian Room, Dumbarton Oaks Museum, Washington

Old man with your cheek drawn into your mouth
after eighty years you have turned to yourself at last
to taste. There's the smell of words that never got out,
a closet of moss growing over their skin walls,
yet because I am not related to you by speech or smile
or memory I do not know what you have stored, saved
between whistling gums when your last
meal dwindles and you take to eating remembered roses.

Old man, someone is kissing you, an old woman in clay
clothes leans to tell you – what?

This or that. Refuse to die. Spit out the pips.
I care for you. You stink like moth-eaten language
and all the curses hung in the airless wardrobe – how you suck them
like lozenges, old man moth
eating cloth. Why are we here? Together,

shelved on glass like layers of clear ice
in the circular sunroom of a museum, our lives
yellowing, we suck our skin and the incredulously
sympathetic stare of those who coming to worship pre-Columbian
stone, onyx, are anguished to recognise the mirrored
self conscious destructive contemporary human.

Saratoga Walk

A fall day in the middle of summer. Time to walk,
cool walk and look at the grasses and the blue, yellow,
white flowers, and steer clear the treasured changing body
from the automobilic. Grass in soldier shapes
that a hand's winding composes into Christmas trees
if you know how from childhood. Rye, cocksfoot, sea-grass
snowgrass, old-gold spear and swords, reeds in the ditch,
ordinary tufted nameless grass anklehigh
in soft strands of wool. Broom or lupin? White
stinkdaisy, royal purple sweet-clover; small convalescent
bees like a new strain survived the insect bomb
suckle the clover head, stagger home
with groceries of brain, only to get the hive going again,
to sting the disaster or build a honeywall against it.
A country's hope lies in its grass wilderness and summer flowers
the outsiders, the disapproved of in marsh, at highway's edge,
– this dark blue hooded flower with its spiked stem
would fight for its existence first by melting hostility
– see – in the blue flame burning in each doorway
of the twenty-five-storey stem.

                              An unfamiliar street
– children playing; plaster animals on lawn and roof, four different
breeds of dog, one with a lion's face. Stars and Stripes
asmack in the quick side-street breeze; maple centurions
where a man could shelter in the hollows;
new leaves glistening with sunlight. Young stripling maples.
Here Doom, not Desire, under the elms. Each year

everywhere their green fountains were rising but not any more.
Stopped not at the source but in midair, a tree-disease
that supposes trees are men; the black skeletons brood in the sky,
cannot be wheeled away or buried like the human crippled or dead.
Elms attacked by a fire no one can see, that begins with a scar,
a stripe like a scorchmark on the body of the elm. A decay
so ripe for a parable it cannot be used, only despaired of
with a guilty – Look what We – not I or they – have done to our land.
Why can we not explain it or cure it before we have learned
with our military foot, our comic-strip tongue, to walk and talk on the Moon?

A bookshop. No customers. An old grey woman peering
at a new bird fallen thirty feet out of its nest. Beak sucking air,
white eye whitening in death. Will you help? Oh no, never,
at least not a direct touch of my shuddering skin on the new puckered flesh.
Use the page of a book, a handkerchief linen, to touch it.
Words are for reading, linen for winding in shrouds, dead birds
for leaving out of sight beyond
our peace of mind and tender appetite. Which book did I buy?
A good story that reads like potion of Life.
Thank God for the grace of the Word but
let God chalk up His own sparrows and elms.

An old part of town. Stone and wood stoops, rocking chairs on the porches.
Rooms to let for racing patrons. Three old women
sit rocking and plotting the deaths of dead kings.
Broadway. The Main Street. Drugstores. Five and Dimes.
A supermarket like a gob stopped with food, insecticide, party favours,
nonfat imitation milk, cookies, Modess, beer, cherry soda,
deodorant, mouthwash, paperbacks, batteries, sneakers.
Newspaper shop with cards: To my dear – to my dearest family
with much love on your automobile accident, fifty cents
with envelope, a popup plaster body inscribed
With Love to your broken foot, arm, leg, head.

A pleasant town of horses and girl students. In August
the Racing Season, concerts orchestral, ballet, film.
Springs with waters healing, mineral, tasting like a fart.
Artists at large. A town where summer light blooms
like a daisy, equal matt and polish of petals in the sky;
a rare butterfly; a hummingbird suspended above a flower
like a word above an idea.
                                  The Underworld growing fat.
Winter. The War. Acres of woods groaning
under the artillery of ice. Crows bark like watch dogs against
the night's intrusion. Boughs,
black coffin-beams nail the infant sky into permanent dark.

Maple Leaves

Maple leaves fall and fade
like old exposed negatives
and none is individual
and none recalls its image.

Maple leaf, what was it you took,
pointed, on fire, towards the light,
metered exactly? Was it
worth the memorial capture?

Here is an album of another year.
None will remember them. Techniques alter.
A picnic, celebration, wedding, christening? Somehow
the light got in and spoiled the picture.

Promise

I will give you a desert swollen with sunburst
I will give you hate and sleep.

I will give you distances that beetles, maggots, bacteria have;
at the same time removing your microscopic eye.

And then, my dear, you will not know where to put
hand foot tongue penis in your walk

towards birth and death, neither feed,
take, touch, out of your welded desperation.

O how the white birches unclothed
lean before the wind! Listen.
The wind is learning to scream.

Today I Cannot Write

Today I cannot write.
At first I said
It is someone over my head
the newly arrived poet
thumping and knocking words out
you'd think with his feet instead
of his typewriter.
               The explanation however
is too simple and neat
and will not fit my perpetual pattern
of excuses.
           Today I cannot write.
That is true.
        Now I say
it is someone under my feet
the grave I walk on where the dead thump and knock
their past out in raucous
blossom headfirst for the communing crows to pick.

For Bill on His Birthday

I shared your childhood too in fantasy
Like the rabbits in your infant drawing,
we both found an underground place for listening
to the too-heavy footsteps of the world.
I knew you, I knew your parents and your grandparents,
though I cannot trace the mysterious source of my knowing.
The privacy of life, the things not talked about;
a poem is an alarm.
The people in your paintings have burned their eyes.
Where is the fire, then? As children we ran fast to the fire
where houses and guys were burned
and the eyes of dolls came out and their arms came off
and their bodies were hollow.

This is a poem for your birthday
(though it's hardly a poem!)
At MacDowell you looked up from your French toast and you said,
                      Oh, is there a piano?

You played the piano for us in the library
while I sat in dark glasses watching your journey.
You said to the music, I give. And, I give up.
I was moved by your journey. So many of us are spiritual stay-at-homes.
You said to Schubert, I know where you are going. I trust you.

Do I presume, on your birthday?
Reste tranquille, si soudain
l'Ange à ta table se décide.

What can I give to you on your birthday?
All my gifts are now negative, the torn-out linings of fantasy
(like those moulted bird-feathers that still shine royal purple when held to the light).
Simply, I would not have you hurt.

In Mexico City

The tourist lies suffering under pressure
the morning cock crows golden and silver
arrows aimed at the sun
return tipped with treasure.
The snake-filled curls of the sun
shake over the sky a gold venom
no centuries of night can suck out.

Stuffed with wallets, silver cockerels, medals,
the tourist flying north by Eastern
tastes the seven o'clock early morning
reality: the small shabby people
wrinkled with sun and worry
who gnaw as a bone the gigantic ingot of history
and go to bed hungry.

Baltimore, November

Down there, now, the season is tightening.
Soon there will be a freeze upon the light.
The kids whose heart-walls are the thudding street
will trail home early, and find nothing to eat.

Silver soda-containers collapse: they have always been frail,
yet they knife the hand, thin-slice the feet,
lie side by side with stars of glass. Kids walk
the concrete night sky with nothing to eat.

The leaves have gone.
Nothing grows fat.
Lungs raid the invisible larder of lead,
mercury, sulphur, free to eat

like tuna sandwich or pear custard.
It's snowing up and down the emergency street,
spurting with raspberry soda blood.
There's too much to eat.

Down Monument Street, Baltimore

How much I learned, walking down Monument Street!
Past the Midget Food Stores, John's Bargain Stores, Monumental Five and
                              Ten Cent, the Salvation Army, Volunteers of America.
Not to mention Eddies, the Veterans.
And then to the Speed Queen establishment to wash and dry the clothes.
I had the place to myself.
The average life of a launderette is eight months.
I remember, way back, when the Speed Queen first opened, and the machines
                                    were shining and attended
and the coke and blue and powder and laundry bag dispensers worked.
And then one day the first machine coughed out cold water instead of hot,
and its neighbour peed like a river on the floor
and someone smashed the coke dispenser and a cardboard notice *Out of Order*
                                      was hung in front of it,
and *Welcome to Your Attended Launderette* became
Welcome to Your Unattended Launderette. Feel free to wash and dry.
I felt free all right. I moved in. The new launderette had opened
a block and a half away

and nobody came any more to be served by the shabbily dying Speed Queen.
Channels of water on the floor; take a chance, a machine might work; nobody
came any more

but one old faithful without washing
who set a machine going for company and sat and watched it
and looked delighted when it switched from hot water to wash to rinse
to cold water to rinse; and when, choking, it stopped,
his face showed a moment of shock as if the machine had died.

By now the windows of the building were all broken.
At night the hoods set to work.
One morning *your unattended launderette open twenty-four hours*
a day feel free to wash and dry
had one washing machine wrenched from the floor. The coke dispenser had
dispensed itself.

Then the notice:
Launderette closed. Opening shortly two blocks away your wonderful
Cold Water Wash. Your own attended launderette.

That was that. Eight months' life.
And the old man, sick with drugs or hunger,
still waiting for someone to open the door.
Twenty-five cents is cheap enough for good company.

The Legend

Chickadees as if grey-feathered with a blue rinse
flock for crumbs. I feed them cinnamon treats and sour milk.
The day ends with the sun going down
in a stream of urine-coloured light.
Shadows thicken in the woods; the tree-trunks
black and white like newsprint decay suddenly
showing the yellow of extreme youth and age.
Swallowed by the sun the leaves are excreted.
The old incontinent trees unintelligibly
announce the disaster.

I and they are alone here.
My bed is made on the pathetic track of their fallacy.
I leave out food for creatures I never see who never eat it.
I walk in the woods hoping to find

copperheads or rattlesnakes among the granite boulders;
a bobcat, black bear, raccoon, woodchuck;
not understanding my own persistent hopefulness.
When noon sun drops in assorted shapes like broken yellow plates
I think Now, especially now, the creatures will come out
but they do not, they do not.

Each morning the woods are still, woven with strand of light,
the trees emerging like a promise kept – to be and stay,
none absent or lost
though with perhaps a new layer of spruce-needles, maple leaves,
birch, aspen scattered like time-dust on the forest floor.
There are bird-sounds like a cat lapping milk.
A woodpecker knocking. Leaves crackle like footsteps in the sky.
A tree walking? Crackling of boughs, rustling, the evidence of parcelled secrets.
I stare and stare into the woods, seeing only
a trapped army settling in for a long siege
its preoccupations and secrets military
its concern uncalmed by memory.

I wanted quietness. I have it.
The blood in my head has licence to speak. Outside,
crows and blue jays survive, are therefore unwanted,
are never at a loss for speech, never unheard,
while the trees are sighing like a sea so distant I shall never look on its waves,
a sea out of memory. The trees that stay,
that lose yet keep what they lose,
what have they to speak of when the wind blows but their life-place and loss,
their struggle to breathe the polluted air,
the animals' desertion and death? Yet their hope is high,
as high as the flames of their fiery leaves.
I could strike them for their stupidity, their martyrdom, their patience.
Nothing else, except ice, has such patience.

Flocks of small birds like newly-discovered opinions
suddenly sway back and forth and vanish
in a rush of wings. Silence. A barking crow
kennelled somewhere in the treetops cries Unchain me.

Overhead the arrogant planes speak
free-ranging like the lost buffalo herds
doing their faithful metal service, cabin, tail, nose-cone
replacing hide and horn.
None dare speak against them.
They draw the world together.
They make nations so close,
as close as neck is to tightened noose.

(Crows with their persecuting cry…)

Noon. A wind rising. Yellow leaves falling.
The view cross-purposed with colour,
life and death – if you need to keep splitting existence.
(Lie low in the prison of granite walls
ticktock the crystal message tetrahedronal.)

I will steer clear of treasure, rubies and bullion.
Not wanting the thing itself which is too hot to handle
I'll take as leaves the sunburned negatives of innumerable
killing snapshots blood-spilling in these mountains and valleys,
and thus bypassing the usual fire and treasure I'll reach images of blood,
preserve an album of autumnal woods,
a world in shadow and the sun looking over my shoulder.

A populated fairyland, every inch a fantasy?
(Day darkens. Sunlight shows
in points like parking lights between the trees.)
These woods alone preserve the legend,
and these huge granite boulders flung from glaciers where there are no longer
glaciers

where there is only anger, anger
at the fairytale's dissolution.

Martha's Vineyard

1

Look out of the window at the sea riding high
sweeping in some movement that is not market, fashion, people or automobiles
in downtown Manhattan or on paper graphs. Is it blood
flowing in on full tide putting annihilating pressure upon the heart-shell?
Who will bother to listen to your sand? A windgift only
to doubleblind the blind eyes.

Martha's Vineyard. The fruit always ripe. Sun and moon treading the seaflow
brimming into goblets of coast. Let it be known it is a good year for tears and
common salt –
a vintage year. Drains in, seeps out. A drunken directionless land
growing also grape-shot while I, Martha, in the steel vineyard cannot determine
which way the War is blowing.

Rain clears. The possibilities grow
thick as poison ivy, cling like ticks upon the expanse of light.
We will row boats, swim in the pool, drink wine,
contemplate our bloody luck and the trees that still stand but did not survive.

2

The boy in the basement steers a spacecraft into heaven.
What is heaven? The flowering of the summer squash
in his small garden; a rack of carpenter's tools; two gerbils;
a walk on the sand
hand in hand with his father
who conjures the great white whale out of print
into the ocean within a few yards of the house.

It is his mother gently disentangling his unhurt fingers from Charlotte's web;
the morning ride on the punt to Chappaquiddick;
nurses and children; the private beach;
the best; white;

white whale and cloud.
Two or three feet taller where
adults turn their heads to say No,
it never happened, look who's winning the game,
which ghost passed like a storm down the highway,
heaven though nearer is further away.

The best; white; white whale and cloud off Nantucket.
And the web of the everlasting sea-mist
and the dark eyes of the coming winter
creeping in on its six claws for the kill
and the tiny ticks – you stoop from heaven to pick them off –
getting their fill of blood.

My son my son feeding on my flesh; the best;
white whale and cloud the webbed sea-mist
the warm purple summer, the gold
grass with the sun shining through
the skin of the sky stripped by lightning,
the Atlantic at war in a far off age of thunder.

Moss

The Spring moss
the plush lining of the jewel-box
rediscovered beneath the snow.
Fever-green surfacings.
Ice with its edges smoothing
shaping in the lick-tongue of the sun
transparent white-green sweet;
then – moss as renewal, a green extra,
sun-sweat, the flower-in-itself, starry evidence,
incapable of wounding.
Spring-moss, crib-moss, beginnings.

Now, forlorn green light upon the black trees,
the moss of neglect, decay, weather,
the aftermath of a yearlong feast
with the year gone suddenly away.
The day has cut off the heat and the light.
Wind snarls in the rain O poor groaning mouth
at the crevices of a season shot full of holes
by birch and maple fire, the trees' incredulous
It does not happen here, the violence of desertion,
of the difference between our lives as mosscovered graves
and the source, the mine of rich leaflight.

Newly unexpectedly ancient
the trees weep in their mossy beards
in the desolation of rain and cold
in the disillusion of a colourfast world's fading.
Only the angel birches, good with weather,
receive violence, return grace.

A Pearl of Oblivion

I smell something dead. I search among
the rain-soaked leaves and pine-needles for the body.
I know the smell of death. I can find nothing, no creature.
In front of my studio, then, there's the dead smell,
and at the back, the gas leaking from my private sewer –
the bread of death making a sandwich of golden air and light
where I, some kind of bacterial filling, try to write.

Mosquitoes hang around, hover hoping against hope.
The rain and the leaves drip-drop. A low blue mist
blurs the distant trees across the field. Another week,
two weeks and all the gold will be marked down, going cheap,
and then, thank God, the Midas craze will be over.
I'm living in a postcard. Let me out. The town houses
are too proud and beautiful, white-painted, three-storeyed;
the children are blonde angels, the sky is blue, the light golden.
Here's the gold that has bought the privilege of pure air,
privacy, more trees than people, the Country Club,
the Golf Course, Huntsmen out shooting the deer.
                    Go away gold light
go home return to your fantasy country.
Here among the boulder-relics of the Ice Age
water flows as the accomplished machinery of the morning world
in a land of graveyards – how else make use of the granite?

Gold light, you make us hungry, you are the 'goldenbrown'
of carefully baked food, the ripe fruit, the roast in the oven done to a turn,
the crust and toast of the season, not fire or flame,
but the recognition of being ripe, our own memory of ripeness,
of leaves and lives rotting away with pride, without shame, at harvest.
'Leaves are not actually green but yellow. They contain
chlorophyll and a special material called anthocyanin...'
The local *Evening Sentinel... Transcript...* explains it
explains it away.

Rain rains in the woods. The big parasol leaves
of the younger trees flip and flop.
I can't stop staring and listening –
the correct attitude for crossing a road full of murderous traffic.
(There are ferns like jagged rows of decaying teeth.)
It's a crowded highway if you count the leaves using it,
the flashing amber and red lights
and there's enough violent death to satisfy the statistician
until next year when the toll
will be comparable.

I sit here as if in a city café looking out of the window
at the leaves and people going to their graves of conference and love.
The rain is over. It is noon.
The cicadas have struck a knitting melody,
a shawl of sound, a shroud to be put by until
the earth is quiet enough to measure the exact need.

Sun controls with its shining, the air is warm, mellow
except for that stony glint of ice
a northern pearl of snowy light
coated with oblivion.

The Birch Trees

Mysterious the writing on the birch-bark
a tune of growth with hyphenated signature,
coded rolls a pianola might play,
a computer accept as mathematical formulae,
surrendering the answer, the question lost.

They tell me the birch tree is delicate
they tell me so often I believe it.
I have seen birches like grey rainbows washed of colour
arched beneath the storm
backbending not breaking,
and the young trees their stick-limbs announcing
all deficiencies beside the one prolonged
nourishment of survival.

Birch trees need never ask: Why are we here? They know.
Opportunity trees, their business is the beautiful
disposal or draping of weather
especially of snow distributed across their
grey branches in such a way
their bark becomes a calligraphy of scars and stars.

Reading it suddenly in the woods one is astonished
to find engraved on pages of birch-bark the fiction
and fact of men in their cities.

Calypso

Annie Francis Annie Francis
turned into a hermit crab
with red painted fingernails
stole the palace I died in
where the ceiling received the rain
the hurricane crumbled the pearly gates.

I'm serving whelk and conch
I'm crying out for independence
I'm playing guitar and drums.

Come back come back little hermit crab
you'll never be able to cross the sandy sky
to drink the coconut milk at the end of the coral rainbow
without a violent breaking of your shell
by the earliest bird
the black and yellow striped bird of morning.

Letter from Lake Bomoseen

Dear Frank, after twenty-five years and my first letter from Ibiza,
Calle Ignacio Riquer, catalogue of starved cats,
tumbleweed, almond blossom, blinkered horses on a treadmill
drawing water from the deepest well – it is true that only concentration,
enforced darkness will help in reaching the clearest water...

After all those jersey-and-skirt years
I write now from Lake Bomoseen to where you, with Persil,
may be sitting on the verandah trying to link some worthy dream of the perfect
sentence
that will offer you a place between the letters
of words you deal honestly face upward. Do you sit,
encircled by the sentence as it protects you in return
– was there ever a 'return'?

You taught me never to suppose I knew
what characters thought,
to take the absolute point of view
like the housefly.

Here it snows night and day, the size of the flakes changing
say those who know, with the temperature.
The warmer the air, the larger the snowflakes
like tissues come home to the two dickeybirds upon the wall,
which gives the least
ever-after before sleep.

Has it, as the poets say, come to this?
A handful of ash after fire,
a scoop of sand after the stone mountain,
a concentrate to which add the immensity of life gone...
or is it the best expansion, the traveller free of ingots,
with skin of golddust
dazzling, brilliantly illuminating the boundary
and – ah! Burdened states of disease,
the ease of crossing!

The Sick Pawpaw

Hideole old cripple pestered
with crime-fibres of thirst and fever
winding strangling your infertile body
your stem, your sick backbone their spool
to weave your envy of monkey-apple, snowberry,
seven-storey beanflower with bees and sun
early sweeping the white carpet, drift
and pile of pollen on the black stairway;
of soldering bolt of orange and lemon fruit
melting, moulding the dark
poured like winterfall to fit your shape
alone, rocking hopeless helpless in Eden
snake-bitten Hideole old cripple
knowing malice, death, weaving the sack
to steal your fuel from orange and lemon, burn
the snowberry and the beautiful tall stairway.

The Family Silver

The glacier, ancient family silver
melted, flowed
from mountain to mountain
to assist in the upkeep
of geological time.

The animal granite, crouching low,
suddenly dazzled out of its white bed
remained profitably stone
resold the State of New Hampshire
for a song, a green song.

Pelted down green rain
restoring the time-tarnished
unrecognisable plate
to silver bowl and spoon
set out for forests to dine on snow and flame.

Bouquet

After five days the snow cannot bear its own silence.
The lion avalanche begins to roar,
springs from the roof to kill.
Burial is no problem.
The polished casket of night arrives too late.
Snow has even arranged
the smallest details that matter
– the strewn lilies with the indecipherable signature.

Snow

Suddenly on this unnatural morning
in a soundless avalanche of light,
snow is committed, suffocating,
gradually making numb the dazzled buildings,
and the people crunching past, giant-shadowed and vivid,
in seeming innocence of evil.

Yet here is evil. Here is famine,
the crumb of bread entombed in the grain of wheat,
the wheat wound in the white sheet.
Here is fire – the pure momentary paralysis
between what shall be and what was,
the madness that makes the murderer go
like snow with a hate-bladed sword
to commit the coldest form of sleep.

Here, too, is reprieve.
Hansel and Gretel in the wood
deep, lost, yet not entirely lost
while the crow Night beats his wings against the snow.

Let a Fox Come By and the Porcupine Night Shine with Starry Icicles

Now the fiery leaves are lying low
crunch like pale biscuits under my feet
the birch-bark, its code complete
unfurls upon the interpreting wind.

A few maple leaves still flare against the sky.

The routine of the woods today is:
All morning, stillness. Afternoon:
Let a storm come in, under, through.
Bury the recent dead. Wear brown and grey.
Also, sigh as if full of care.

Evening: Let a fox come by, and the porcupine night
shine with starry icicles.

The Real Porcupine Night

The real porcupine night is black
wears icicles and golden quills
and when it walks it writes a shiver of light
from jewels set within the golden quills.

The real porcupine night with its reptile's tail
will thresh giant maples to dust
scar-slash birches innocently growing to crystalhood
from their seed-bed of snow.

Secretive, defensive, barb of time sunsprouting tomorrow,
the real porcupine night is a creature you will never see or know,
is out of reach of the conspiracy
of the human eye and light, the murdering spectrum.

The Crows

In the early morning the grass is a swirl of smoky blue.
The hump-backed shadows melt. The wax dark
trickles down the sky and lies at the foot of the trees
receiving the warm impression of sun.
The harvest is light. Rat winter, invading
the granary, will gnaw the golden seed.

I fancy the urge of leaves to live
has changed many to yellow butterflies and moths
still signing their doom with their passion for light,
beating like the prematurely buried out of their graves.

The crows choke on their own wild cry.

The Chickadee

The chickadee drops like a scroll out of the sky,
alights on my hand. I feed him sunflower seeds.
The inky brushmarks on his head are scarcely dry.

5

Weekend

I had forgotten about the sea here in the city
where people uttering no cry disappear
day by day in quicksands of iron; and gulls
black-backed rapacious dive through smooth
plate-glass waves to retrieve plastic fish
swimming on bright streamers; where the high tide
of five or six o'clock casts to shore
the stray drift and wreck of commerce, men
torn each day from the shrunken eight-hour breast
of their foster sea. I say I had forgotten.
Lately the days have been warm. We are drowsed
like flies in a spider-web of sun. The coast lies
like a dazzling tossed plait of mulberry silk.
I had forgotten the city. But the picnickers came
like rainbow balloons swelling with ozone and ice-cream
each moored to a claim pegged out with basket and flask
and tartan rug in the sand. Then the traffic of sea
never stopped. Gull-shoppers beaked through wave doors of ripple
for litter displayed in the salt colossal sale.
Until at six o'clock the pub-like but always unquenching
green sea closed its doors to the drift of men.
They lay dead. I found them heaped in shape
and twist of seaweed, suckling the iron sand.

Eater of Crayfish

Commonplace, divine, bald, at home,
licking day-long breath from the walls of his air-cell
he will eat the crayfish green-garnished in its blush of dying,
burned, like love, in and beyond the salt element.

He will taste the embarrassment of dying,
tear off the livid armour hiding the bloodless flesh,
destroy the cable laid along the sea-bed
communicating bloom of excrement.

From the time he is born he will need to eat this crayfish,
his left hand love, his right hand hate, he will take
larger and larger meals of nightmare till his life accumulates
eyes, eyes, that walk on twigs under the sea.

Storms Will Tell

Storms will tell; they can be trusted.
On the sand the wind and high tide write
bulletins of loss, imperfect shells,
by smooth memorial of high-country trees,
sea-weed, ripped bird, fine razor, ramshorn, cockleshell.

Give us the news say the tall ascetics reading
ten miles of beach over and over; between empty shells, look,
burning from the salt press, stories
of flood: How I abandoned house and home.
Razor: How I slit the throat of sunlight.
Ramshorn: How I butted and danced at the ewe sunlight.
Cockle: How my life sailed away on a black tide.

Winter

It is the worst winter I have ever known.
The cold, coming to liquid, solid life
has poured through the cracks in the walls and the holes in the ceiling,
set like glacial rock in every room.
This winter I have not been resident in my house. Had you called
you would have noticed frost and ice were most at home.

There has been no other winter in my life, it seems
only this winter past. Outside
the frost-scarred daffodils
have broken out in sores instead of buds;
and a stranger came, pruning (he said) and chopped off
the right arm in its green sleeve of my favourite tree.

I cannot believe in the sun.
Healing and warmth do not happen any more.
Snow is knives, not petals or feathers.
The frost will never again crack open the perished seed.

To be surrounded, walled in by one season only,
now and forever while the granite Southern Alps, the mountain chain, the
                                                    backbone
quietly paralyse the nerve of summer
lock all doorways leading to the rumoured sun.

Oh I know the commonplaces – how the aged fight to keep their life
and yet surrender it to the season they conquer
when the season itself is dead; how July and August are
the enactment of the last scene of *Hamlet* – 'Exeunt bearing off the bodies' –
and the drums are starlings waking, and thrushes;
oh even the spring children, not birds, are breast-spotted with measles.
Childhood is crocus morning, snowdrop noon, ear-ache night.

Why must this year take command over all winter dreams and memories?
Must I forget the snow piled high against the wall of the mansion
last year, in Saratoga?
the return of the scarlet tanager and the humming-bird?
the black king-snake waking by the waterfall
the wetskinned leaves hovering delicate as bats' wings
the snap-turtles rising out of the mud, the shining striped muskrat
swimming fast for life and love through the lake-water;
and the butterflies unreturnable, freakborn from a certain happy setting of sun
                                                                              and air

an embarrassment of brilliance
ornamentations like the flourishes on the signature of Spring?
Am I not allowed to remember other winters that died
with a happy ending?
                        In childhood
I found frost and ice good.
Thin ice cracked when I stamped on it. I picked and ate
the frozen dew lying on the cabbage leaves
and the raindrops too slow to get away
trapped solid along the tops of the fences.
My feet stamped stamped; iron sting
of skipping and clear ring of steel voices around the moon,
and always, forever, some other creature providing the fire.

The dead are cold. The sun shines fiercely.
The dead with ashwhite faces lie in the furnace
immune to the chemistry of flesh and metal
unlocking preparing their new code of not-being, fusion and blossoming
beyond and above recognition. Shine fiercely, sun,
but not so fiercely as to burn
the new and nameless.

Compass

Once I was overtaken by
geometry: a golden compass lying
in a silver box that had cutting edges
and sliced through my finger – if
you had to choose would you be
the centre or the foot of the compass?

– the short foot harnessed to a dainty pencil
with nothing to do all day but describe
describe the perfect circle and
meet your origins foot to foot on a highway
narrow enough to contain you only
or would you rather pierce what you touch
putting out who knows what eyes of light
sharp deep stay-at-home as balance, reference for
the wandering – no, rather the successfully striding – foot?

But if you are a compass have you really a choice?
Are you not wholly – stay-at-home and traveller – *It*?
I think I'd rather be the wide-open measured mouth of
the radius tasting every drop of distance.

The Landfall Desk

Desk, your *Landfall* people segmented within the drawers,
your sides battered, knocked at by writers wanting to get out and into Print,
your body sawn in half and rejoined, your toes cut off,
you squat in the middle of the room
you don't dare to attack now with your sharp corners
the passing literary aspirants breathing their cherished syllables.
You malicious, magnificent-mileaged one-owner desk,
you were kind in your time,
used kindly, too,
were never at the mercy of a mad shifter of furniture
trained for the secondhand kill, bred among giraffe pianos
and minute waltzes, quite mad, mad among the mahogany and walnut.

I think I will keep you, malicious desk.
You refuse to stay tidy, you get stuck and you wobble on your cut legs.
The edges of the wound around your middle
will never meet again; you are unbalanced, overweight.

I remember the day I took you in,
a Dunedin day of generous cloud
– no niggardly blowaway tufts in these journeying skies
pursuing their massive somewhere along a one-track wind from the mountains
to the sea

towards the north, the Peninsula and beyond.
There was some suggestion that day, I remember, that I remove my front door
to admit you.

It was not necessary. How agile you were, how accommodating, how fitting!

You were something to live up to.
Perhaps, after all, something I could never face –
too good, too clever, too correct.

Mind my reputation, you said, when I dropped the wrong word or touched you
with a misplaced syllable.
It was later, I remember, that your corners began to attack me as I walked by you.
Once, during my absence, the occupants of the house dismembered you and hid
you in the cellar until I returned.
I would never have known except for the white-faced literary person who beckoned
me in the street one day

– You can't guess what they did! Her horror was clear.
– What did they do?
– I don't know how to tell you.
– Tell me.
– They took it to pieces. It was too big. The room couldn't take both the desk
and the double bed.

I was calm. I knew.
– You mean, I said, The Landfall Desk?
I thought she was going to faint. The Landfall Desk!
– How dreadful, I said, without meaning it. I was curious, though, about its
battle with the double bed,

its assertion, – There isn't room for both of us.

Eight-legged, a kind of spider secreting, out pouring your daily web,
a mad, crooked, crippled piece of furniture,
bathing in golden literary history,
in spite of all, you go with me, Landfall Desk, kept,
endured, burrowed in by the blossoming alphabet
in spite of all, in my shifting life, you go with me...

On Not Being There

Nothing, no one at the door. The fuchsias are not healthy this year.
Their bruise-colours not healed into blossom, their burned-varnish
seed-purses empty. The polyanthus, transplanted,
that Margaret gave me, droop, wind-trampled, hit too, cut
by the rolled paper-bag thrown over the hedge by the rag-dealer. Also, the
                                                                    once fiery
geraniums are small as wild-sweet peas uncolour-fast
against the swish of east coast rain.
Why should Pluto stand at the door then? I'm not Persephone,
I've not even flowers to rival his jewels. Besides,
I'm willing.
            'An inaugural concert is being given on the new Steinway
to an invited audience.'

Black sleeping Steinway, underworld God,
sending your special representative to me, inviting me
(only in phantasy).
How did they choose who would hear your first word?
And, today, are you now inaugured?
And what did the specially invited audience feel and think, and,
last night, how did it sleep and dream?

And the Steinway? Surprised, attacked by a lover (the usual comparison)
    murmuring with its handfinished voice, I didn't know I had it in me,
its dream-self replying, It was given you,
the argument ensuing,
I gave it, I remember now, I invited the hands, the fingers to touch,
it was a spell I cast and cannot help.
How strange my newness is, my foreignness, my awkward beautiful shape. It
                                                                    took three men
to bring me home to a home I did not choose,
and I've slept standing up, canvas-blanketed like a madman
from whom violence is feared, and sometimes, slyly,
student finger-tips have lightly touched my mobile
black and white bones
that give renowned agility to my stay-at-home body.
Literally, my heart is in my mouth!
My polished skin ensures tranquillity
to all that gazes in me – I reflect lights, walls, faces, I reflect the reflected
            light of the sun shining through that tall window and through
                        the blue gauze panel of soundless daylight.
Sun has no noise: it is I make the noise of sun. When the sun peers into my skin
                it swells with golden silence, all light is at peace then
until hands and their fingers begin the restless searching for the world-noise

I have since birth, naturally stolen. Dare to approach me. Your sound that you
                                        cannot hear, is mine. Do not ever be afraid,
it's only the possibility of my natural speech.
You too speak through your bones, but you walk and run and unite.

Here, in this hall, my stand is permanent as if I had taken root
and will flower – you will admire my blossoms –
in the kind season.

I will tell you about last night since you were not there,
not being an important person, that is, one who contributed
or one who would benefit, or one able socially to jostle and smell nicely
as if you had just had a bath. (Malice creeps in, I fear.)
First, they removed my canvas blanket and stood back, fearfully,
sensing my passion for destruction, thinking it directed at them
and not as musical furnace consuming the noise-refuse, the offcuts of cries,
even the almost indestructible remnants of the swish of passing stars,
and the enormous still-born foetus of silence;
so they stared, afraid, not comprehending the source or
diction of my passion. Had it been love also (which it is)
they would have feared as greatly.
Undressed, how I was polished again, and admired, and the sly fingers of
                                        strangers touched me, guiltily,
as if hands were caressing a thigh, in darkness.
I speak whenever a hand touches me, you know. I'm a speak-easy.
I'm a sing-hard, for most I'm a make-music-impossible.

Next, these attendants removed or opened one wall of my skin,
propping it up like a trapdoor, peering inside, and again,
guiltily fingering. With my bone-eye I witnessed
rage in one face, the rage of not understanding yet wanting to, and I heard one
                                        man say,
– It's the first concert tonight. Going?
– Bloody well not. Give me –
But I forget what he wanted to be given. Some particular personal heaven.
– All set? Right.
They patted my flank as if I were a fine breed of horse,
I shuddered to hear
the door slammed fast again
on my aloneness. I began to feel apprehensive, chilled. My black
feet froze in their roots. I felt a sigh from a secret heart move
between my keys. My newness came to me, as all sensations come,
in a tide of sound, a raw brown wave that grazed my machine-made, hand-tuned
                                        senses. I think I slept then,
and when I woke my stillened bones seemed to have
a thousand lights like water running down upon them and I heard
the special noise-refuse of people wearing layers of

clothes and carrying used voices in their mouths and the
door to my bones was opened and a hand touched them
as if the light on my bones were the shine on a cat's fur.

You know the rest, if you read your morning paper.
The pianist played with his usual etc. etc. Tone-colour. Brilliance.
Written words encircling what I had been, like a word-web.

Bach

This music never was or will be,
is insistently Now; yet out of reach
not as reward or promise unfulfilled or planet
unconcernedly exploding out of earshot
but as sound that, rarely in music, makes no excuses
does not stand or rise from any human ground
exists in its own foundation and pinnacle
may be spun upside down and retain perspective and balance in itself
while the inner ear of the listener suffers the sickness
of being out of element yet compelled by a celestial gravity
to touch the shapes of ideas as if their sound deep in an advancing tumult
of black mineral forests were a strange dark blue and grey stone vegetation
arranged precisely with transparent ice flowers...

Bach: the same old story...
He can argue with the sun
and win while at the same time
the sun quietly releases its overflow of light
to the moon keeping track of the human night.

He can make a mathematician turn pale
by going beyond the nth power.
He is also a very good carpenter
a passionate driver in of nails
until you might think he is trying to crucify
the cathedral he seeks to build; and he is, and does,
and the nails are fire
with phoenix sound triumphant in the glittering spire.

Bach: the same old story; things celestial, Angels and Co. by
very special delivery.
Why?
His music is certainty. It is stern without compromise.
It reveals a man who refuses to suffer in silence.

Without his telescopic vision his transport genius
which arranges a multitude of journeys between earth and heaven
cloud-commuting on several tracks without collision
Bach might be, say,
a musical gossip
writing an aural manual of fucking positions
between man and silence
which may or may not be called God.

Schubert

Schubert:
switch on the radiator
human beings must be kept warm
open the window on the unattainable heaven
– Schubert is home.

He has brought the gift of perfection
the melody of feeling
of despair yearning sitting on a bed of roses,
of warm bliss, like a child, full of dreams and wishes
(before children were found out of their innocence),
lying asleep on the rain-rotted boards of a prepared grave.
From the laboratory of the living-room
he can get round anything even death with a melody
his musical chemistry.

At the Opera

The great opera singers
lay musical notes like eggs
speckled with words
or words speckled with musical notes
that hatch in the ear
as the audience sits
in the velvet room
tier on tier
tear on tear
looking grim.

Sometimes the egg falls and is broken
and the listening people smile
yellow and red
with blood and sun
or frown frown
at the white secretion

and when they go home
tier on tier
tear on tear
looking grim
they make love with double alarm
and multiple charm
with their bones singing
like tuning forks
and their egg-shaped eyes
hatched out and flying
through the day and night skies.

Words Speak to Jakow Trachtenberg

(who devised his arithmetical system during his seven years as a prisoner in a concentration camp)

Because you were a calculating speaking man
a literate numerate man
we came, your servant words,
to attend your breaking heart in its darkness.
Among us there were ten strangers wearing uniform,
and though our roots pleaded, Examine us, grow, destroy, at least touch us,
the strangers did not speak or plead.
Night and day we and they came to attend your suffering.
Some of us died or were changed,
some were needed most
to dress the Prince of Genocide in polished armour,
to feed honey gathered from the flower of death
to those who could not grasp the fact of the deed.
We, your servant words, prepared ourselves to bear the weight of your anguish
to build your sanctuary city- or world-wide
– were there not enough of us to fill a million rooms of fantasy
to arrange in our special kingdom an inward light to illuminate your darkness
to express hope of the goodness of humankind; and of peace?
Without the touch of your tongue and pen (and you had no pen)
we stayed stillborn, dumb,

while the ten strangers remained clear-eyed, needing nothing, simply *being*,
                                                                      unchanging.

They were solid like stones
but no tears fell on them to stain them
nor did the sun warm them and moss grow on them
yet like stones they were part of the mountainous construction
you built over seven years to shield you from the light of unreason.

We had wings. As we crowded into your cell did you notice our wings?
They had none. They stayed with you. They could not escape
or act as messenger between thought and thought.
They could not move, they had no history.
Simply, *they were*, and could not be killed
while day after day the gas chamber held flesh, spirit and syllable.

You chose the ten as your servants.
You could never have chosen so few of us and lived so freely in your mindwide
                                                                      sanctuary.

Plain guardians, neither faithful nor faithless,
they surrendered to your will and memory,
submitted to arrangement, rearrangement, experiment,
clearing a space in your head between suffering and suffering;
and they stayed with you as parents stay with their child
but without regret or sacrifice.
We servant words have complexity, confusion, fluidity;
we hurt, and eat.
You could hold them safely in two hands at night
like a child's treasure, and sleep.

Threatened with death
you lay your heart upon their cold magnet
their force of life unembellished
by words of hope or promises.
And now you are dead they still exist, your servant numbers,
but they have no memory as we have
and we with our still-living roots and constant blossom
and prefixed eye from time to time see one of the ten: we remember and flower
petal and heart, for we can speak,
we embrace their silence and tell their pattern
as, say, ten birds on the wire
ten drops of water in the pool,
ten stars jagging the darkness,
ten prisoners trying to distil and count
the grains of salt in their tears.

These Poems

These poems that ripen
in the orchard and drop rotten

popularise, go through fire and water;
bleak, remarkable,
work, make out, make do.

Tincture of light
spooned momently to the eye
I, blind, a traveller in surfaces
ask me ask a fly or beetle
to design your highway where
wheels burn, sing, burst; free
seven-year retread for the foot
silk-slippered with skin.

Return to the orchard, supposing
it bloomed at the end of the garden. New trees not ready
to bear fruit have yet been fed by god good god
with hormones, all planned ahead; in the autumn
wordpickers with baskets, ladders,
stay all day, come home in the evening
with golden fruit, eat it and are sick
with diarrhoea from temptation in desert and orchard
the payoff a sentence
stopped by a stone
bruised tongue and foot; it is the stillness
of the body
measures the coffin.

Arrival

Paged at the airport I pick up the red telephone.
The voice speaks, I've come to meet you.
I am distinguished by my height, colouring of hair and clothes,
no visible scars.
I shall wait in the lobby. Remember, the doors open and shut
with electronic judgement, untouched by human hand.
There's no hope for you if you change your mind,
you are cut in half vertically
– it happened to me!

I put down the red telephone. Nothing to pay, no nickel or dime,
only to plan a rearrangement of my exit. Come in, get out,
the doors invite, reject.
Between the invitation and the rejection
falls the electronic decision.
Easier for amoebae than for people
to suffer such division.

A Year at Home

1

Time to take notice once more
of old places and passions,
to pierce the centre with one foot of the compass
and world-circling the arm, suck stars in and the sun;
time to nourish grow and burn.

The city newly infested with dollars
the complaining people shouldering the weather;
within the wider loneliness the foretaste of loss
and a thought for the dead who will miss the September blossom.

Turning simplicity
the weathervane above the seven hills,
the hills like compressed woodsmoke.
Beaks of yellow broom, lips of gorse;
sweet perfume except
the taste of today and tomorrow.

The stars and the sun come in
and the beatnik moon skycombing.
The lightwaves drown,
the tide of daylight breaks down sight and flesh
to sand: here the long lonely home beach
and the wild peninsula, the wind sharpened at ocean-edge.

2

A year at home.
Time to slip into the poetic chariot
beat out the course upon upgraded metaphors;
and the whole world on holiday
saying to the snow take my foot in frostbite

but O suggest, flake or mower-blade
an offering place for the heart!

A country with toothache
and a deadened mouth.
Clove-sweet the summer
the anaesthetic dollar.

3

Time at home
among the officials and workmen who tell of their private lives.
Liberty to walk in deserted streets, to trust, smile,
forget the passport and flight number
the crosstown peril, the uptown downtown terror.

Not so many and not so many sick here:
there the pale drowned faces rise like dreams in the street
reminding,
            If the swing of the compass encircles the stars and sun,
the mellow hills, the blossom,
even the dead rusty and stiff as old garden rakes,
then why not us
who cast a bigger shadow than a star?

Clean-plunged in the green home lawn
the compass foot pierces the city's abscess
the downtown waste spilled on the summer doorstep.
Time in a year at home to speak to the murdered or drowned faces
                              rising rising
disbelieved at the banquet
to brood on the truth, the disaster
of the sun's equal shining.

Talk of Economy

Talk of economy – butter, cheese, raised lakes
the drowned bodies of trees,
oil, seamen, soccer, sulphothion,
brood mares, rugby football,
champion heifers and shearers,
rates, Plunket, opera, aluminum shares,

100

enemies, allies, special powers and preventatives,
grass grubs, classrooms, black widows, paraplegic
games, apartheid, radioactive bathing in the South Pacific,
casinos, whales, coalmines, demolished churches, free
concerts of twentieth century music, how to fill the Dunedin
Town Hall without using a dentist's drill. Talk,
talk in a fairly literate country, stepping up
the pace of words conveyor-belted on the tongue,
back and forth from 'contemporary scene' to
'viable present-day situation'.

It was I think, at the other side of words the escape was made,
beyond the conveyance of faces and conveyancing
the settlement of the property of smiles, speech, tears
and all the other chattels of human features.
It was at the other side, beyond colour and image.
                                    The dead are resting,
bathed only in rest. The custom is not, not
to take off the clothes of living for inspection and removal,
the accumulated treasure, and go naked into nothingness;
the custom is not a capture and surrender; it is a sudden or
slow enfolding of life by rest. Wrap up warm, contain the sun,
sleep unafraid, in peace, in the wordless night.

If I Read St John of the Cross

If I read St John of the Cross, I lose heart,
there is nowhere to hide.
Everything is too difficult.
I know that I suffer from 'spiritual gluttony'
I cannot remain still.
I must contemplate creation and the creator and praise him.
He is unknown, unknowing.
I agree with St John of the Cross that all things known and felt
and imagined must be cast out as useless in the contemplation of
the Lord God. I keep hanging on the edge of imagination of Him, trying
to reach a knowledge that by its definition is non-knowledge of
Him.
Yesterday I went to the Church and was the only person there. There
was a storm. The wind howled and wailed, the window panes high up
rattled. It is a new church, made of beautiful wood inside. I thought

the workmen did an imperfect job on those windows high up; they
should not shake and rattle in the storm. They could fall out, and
harm a passer-by. Why do workmen not work with all their might.
Christ may have belonged to Boons the contractor, as a carpenter,
labour only. He would have put the windows in the correct
way so they would not be affected by the storm. The divine perfection.
I should be humble and consider my imperfections.

Thank the Lord for all good things, for the goodness of living
and for the world about me; and for answered prayers.
I will go to the house of worship no matter what denomination it may
be. Hear my prayer.

Tourist Season

The beating land grows older. The people crowd
like blood against the slowly hardening walls;
camp too close, more neighbour to their known
heart than any fly-by-night retired
American, lone fisherman, tourist stranger
rich with the day's takings where the rainbows end.

Is it the retired man from the farthest end
of the world, he whose thigh-boots thick as trees crowd
the numb lonely limbs of sand, or, over the sea wall
tide-leaping twice a day, the salt unknown
other tourist, Pacific, Tasman, no waves too tired
that will warm the coast whose own blood is a stranger?

The sea cries its chorus, Who is the real stranger?
Is it he who clamps his own pulse from dawn till day's end?
Who sprawls upon his heart, who crowds
in partnership with self and self against the walls
of roaring cities, who worships the lately known
self outcrop of brick and stone; who, born retired

from his native land, taking rod and line in untired
frenzy to the gold-lapping banks (Taupo a stranger,
Queen Street the pit of sky where rainbows end)
tours like a souvenir among the crowd,
plays his wriggling death across bank-walls,
with the weight of death, the taste and smell sadly foreknown?

The bait in the throat of death is so well known
it deceives. Far on the coast the world-paddling retired
American dazzled with fake flies – Red-Tipped Governor, the stranger
Greenwell's Glory, weighs death at the worm's end,
whistles in the dark of coast where waves crowd
the door of no-where whose house has no brick walls.

So the beating land grows older. Strangeness walls
the distant selves, the boasting, slaphappy, the known
from the afraid, the unknown. The native traveller, retired
from clear vision has no passport in his own territory, is a stranger;
while the terrible fish that never gets away, the certain end
troubles the tourist trampled by a wind and wave crowd.

And only the distant blue coast forgets the walls
of night, is chafed warm, fondled by the untired
salt strangers walking the southern twilight of world-without-end.

On December 31st Each Year

On December 31st each year
Pepys wrote, To my accounts;
as no doubt do our Prime Minister
and others with red and blue line space to spare.

Years ago I was taught arithmetic by shifting counters
to and fro on the desk, button-blue
reds, greens, yellow, worn smooth, a game to play
called *sums*; first, the adding; later, the harder subtraction.

Addicted to writing of occasions, as most writers will tell you they are,
poised for personal and public birthdays, victories, deaths, disasters,
and simple-seeming everyday happenings, I enjoy the celebrations
like Christmas that keep
women in the kitchen, protecting warmed flour from the shock
of mixing with beaten egg – oh the undone baking-powder
naked from its secure wrapping of dry flour
snake-hissing within the whirl…
the celebrations that say it is best to say it is best
to build a feast in the middle of Destroy
when both sides of the street are on fire.

I ramble on
as I am permitted to do
in writing letters of which this is one –
a year-end account of gain and loss
under the bright yellow counter-shifting sun.

Writers died this year – a storm of writers, a sheaf, a page,
a pronoun of writers; we all know their names
and still bleed, saying them, it is strange having to dip writers'
names into their deaths, to coat them with a new
substance
                which makes us say them differently
with a certain mixture of nowhere, somewhere and where
a curious un-knowledge.

We can fix and mix a feasting metaphor
brushing it lightly with their new taste
the new taste of their names and their dust,
we can eat the after-birth of our new cold realisation
a misery-joy mixup, a nourishing Christmas.

It's quiet here today. I've grown to like the light of Wanganui,
the leaves have yearlong a special yellow tint
a starved skin touched up kindly by the sun.
Here, half-way between the city and the sea,
the soil is sand; it chooses which plants it will feed,
slowly destroying others.
At the end of each year I must pull up by the dead roots
the plantings of two winters past.

The pohutukawa, old survivor, blossoms on time,
although the blossoms refuse to look west, seaward.

Pictures Never Painted, Music Never Composed

I learn to start again in the new home,
to relearn the local weather, the prevailing winds,
the direction of the mountains and the sea, which coast
I live nearest.
I had not wanted to start again. The fifteen
years with you in your certainties and uncertainties
calling my tune and yours gave enough company and comfort
for my needs.

104

Well, or ill, you are gone.
You were old, your functions failed, you died with my helping
hand feeding you a butter-coated tranquilliser before the vet came
to finish your life, 'put you down' 'put you to sleep'.

There was no announcement, of course. They buried you, they
said, 'on a farm out of town'.
My neighbour says you were one hundred and thirty, in human terms.
A great age.

And a great life you had, scanning the world and its beings,
second by split second...
Fed on time every morning and evening with the best,
the best.
A vitamin tablet each day.
Your coat brushed and combed.
A house to sleep in, to choose your bed – cushion, chair,
drawer, piled typescripts, box-files, anywhere...
It was your house, shared with me.
You know you were my favourite purr-being.

Between us, there were words from me, and cat-noises answered
by you but always
the torment of unattainable language
words between us would have softened the awful goodbye,
and as we waited for the tranquilliser to work
we might have chatted about living and dying and dying
words the ointment, the bandage.

Instead I sat with you in a barren place
and when I had closed the door of your own home
and watched you, in that cage you hated, put into the vet's car
by someone who never knew you for your fifteen years,
I felt the shock and grief and I said to myself as the seas
froze and the prevailing wind changed cruelly
and I tried to discern the outline and direction of the new coast,
'It happens every day. Animals, people
long loved are lost. Everyone recovers.'

Dear time.

Sometimes Mr Speaker and Blanco Come
to Find If You Are Home

Sometimes Mr Speaker and Blanco come to find if you are home.
They search beneath the oleander and the breath-of-heaven,
the virgilia, the mimosa, the azalea,
among the dead leaves and twigs and dry layers of cut grass;
they snuffle and sniff the scent of your vanishing.
Then slowly, because they are old, they pad across the
road to their own home, their own person
who, limping now, walks with the help of a stick, to greet them.

He asks, 'Well, what did you find over there? Something? Nothing?'

They do not answer directly. Their glance reads,
Absence, absence everywhere, the grass
has sprung up from the nests,
the scent at the tip of the grass-blades is gone.
Nothing is buried in the garden.
No one defended the territory.
The place is open to any cat, any dog,
any rat, mouse or hedgehog.

We tell you, it is a mystery,
a gloomy mystery.

The person smiles and sighs.
Perhaps only the wind in the air is forever.
We're travelling too, with the wind and the stars
and the grass will spring up from our vacant nests.

A gloomy mystery?
We'll see, we'll see.

A Photograph of Me Holding a Cat

I see I have fallen into the trap.
I hold it against my breast
but not on the side of my heart. If you observe closely
you will see my fingers pressed into the fur
of my liable cat my escape-cat who would much rather be stalking
in the great elsewhere at ground or sky level, seldom in between
                                        where people's heads are.
There is a tenderness in the way I balance its back paws on my palm.
I have shaped my arm to fit its body.
It's all quite by chance.
I am frowning hard. I too would much rather be
at my own level where I seldom meet a soul
except perhaps a travelling word or two, hordes of memories,
and because there is a tomorrow, a few meditative dreams
that will accompany me in my pleasurable inward world
my secret mirror of your great here and my great elsewhere.

Lines Written at the Frank Sargeson Centre

Mirrors again. Looking through the surface
diving in to see the under, other world
and, with all, end in the 'green isle',
Auckland perspective from the Euganean Hills?

To be the first fellow, at sixty-two going on sixty-three,
is remarked upon; it's a beginning only, a first gesture, a tuning
for those who follow – perhaps a marking-time,
a treading (in measure) on the grave, with, perhaps of an evening,
a conversation with a neighbouring mentor, a fancied game of chess
using Philidor's Defence.

When I walk here on the upper floor, do you hear my steps
in my Hannah's shoes, thirty-four dollars sixty,
seven and a half American? You are not Sherlock Holmes,
the usual detective. Your skill lies with the Aspern papers,
or a character in Hawthorne. Your investigations
are by syllable.
Do you hear me, as you roam downstairs in the gallery of your centre?

Or, a further storey below, as you cling, a speck of ash
to a tree or flower-root,
going up, going up into the Auckland sun
to inspect your centre?

Your centre.

Is it too much to hope
that after the hard labour of making sentences
into paragraphs and chapters and, finally, copperplate books,
the message of your worth and your work of writing...

Enough,
my old typewriter has grown whiskers like a potato ready to seed,
and its vowels, and the h, d, n and m are clogged with
storms of old ink.

6

The Garden

Yes, there was a garden. Small, overgrown with grass.
A vegetable plot with tall cabbages and silver beet gone to seed.
A moon shining on the garden, its light
lemoncoloured, richly cold.
And there was a plum tree blossoming out of season
the delicate white petals shadowed with blue
like the shadows beneath the eyes of someone loved
who is ill and tired and near death.

The servant came to the small silver-leaved plant growing beneath the plum tree.
He bent down to the plant and put his ear to the leaves
as if he were listening.
Then he watered the plant and went away.
And I knew that the servant's tongue had been buried under the plum tree.

It all seemed so far away
and there was more for me to do than shine my memory upon the other world
for I was not the sun
I could not encompass the wide world in my day's shining.

The Anemone

I the anemone send no messenger to you
make no offer, enticement,
deep in my layer of petals
responding royally, dangerously
to the release of light
I may not even know you exist.

A hint of poison in my stem?
Some early difficulty with my name?
My blue lips that speak of the absence of life?
Why do you need to defend yourself against me?

I do not fall apart readily. I stay put, my mood is vegetable health.
You may buy me wrapped in waxed paper for your graves.
My colour against the tombstones is twilight, winter seas,
some moods of mountains, and distance. You are always arriving at distance.
I move only when the wind moves.
I soon grow tall enough to see my place,

111

the insects, currents of air, seeds, scraps of light
following their beaten path level with my head.
At night I sleep
pulling tight the red and blue curtains.

I was a family flower
bred from an old border cluster
among bonneted grannies, kindhearted Williams, velvet-toothed dragons.
Now, immobile, older, wearing my high green collar
I close my black eye against light I do not understand.

Whatever your passion that persuades me to drink my own bathwater,
that burns the soles of my feet for pleasure,
that puts me among strangers
denies me my world and my weather,
it cannot be, as you insist, love for me and my kind,
though I've heard you say 'I love anemones!'
You love only what you yourself give me. I give you nothing
– perhaps a stained vase, a reminder to feed one of your caged memories.

Make no mistake; I do not complain.
I think, more correctly, you love paralysed reticence,
you must always live close to twilight, winter seas, distance,
enemy,
any moan,
anemone,
to lay your head and mine upon the world's grave.

Freesias

do not need a poem
but have learned with other flowers
to expect a word or two
gracefully in spite of
what poets have been known to commit.

I think sometimes
freesias use too much perfume
the expensive kind
advertise
too many baths, change-daily
O my clean linen.
Always young, always fresh

God for a sour stagnant pool
budding a waterlily.

But it is not right to be flippant
about freesias
or to belittle
the many intoxicated poets who love freesias

I praise their courage
in bearing their essence
from garden to grave
that is, here,
on my desk. And I want

to take the morning world they try to give
(see, I am their victim!)
and the fresh bath of pain
had I not promised not to let pain into this poem
and cannot keep my promise.

Freesias, the giant said,
I smell pain
distilled blood
the essence of rainbows
an innocent
mask of death.

And the giant, nonviolent,
lay down to sleep.

The Earthquake City

What a chance to remantle the deserving shoulders of stone
with the misdeeds of human origin.
How well-dressed the mountains are these days,
how sleek the sea-glitter,
how timely the new-old earth-fashion,
how costly, the diminishing
heart-to-heart of the human account.

The earthquake city was always *theirs*,
a place of makeshift houses, rubble, dust,
theirs too the hunger, the disease, the poverty,

theirs too, the news – they fled carrying all their worldly possessions or
their possessions piled high on an ox-cart.

What horrible places they live in. Isn't it time something was done?
Aren't there *agencies* to right such wrongs? Appeals and so on?

Their earthquake city was part of the news and the photos on TV
the undishevelled reporter brilliantly covering the
total dishevelment.

Today I sing in the undishevelled world
Today in the undishevelled world...

Today from the formerly undishevelled world, I, dishevelled, report
to you the heartache, the tragedy, the compassion.

My neighbour walks by dragging her refrigerator behind her, on a lead.
Another pushes her vacuum cleaner, another carries in her arms her
new food processor.
Trailers of blankets, sheets, warm jerseys.
The end of Kauri Street has become a ravine.

The Bloodless Dead

I was lying alone in a double bed in a strange room.
I could see the anemone-blue mountains outlined against the pearl-grey
morning.
I went barefoot to the window and looked out
at the streets wet and black and starred with frost.
The motorcyclist, Night, his black tunic shining
still leaned against the solid silver lamppost of light.

Then it was morning. I turned from the window.
I brushed my hand against the sill
and the skin of my hand peeled away like paper,
my arms and neck, my face, my whole body had skin of paper,
in the wrinkled places hard like parchment, yellowing.

The woman came into the room, silently, and stared at me.
– You'll never see your own blood.
You'll never get in
beyond your own skin.

114

She clapped her wooden hands together with a hollow knocking sound.
The servant entered. He put shoes on my feet, combed my wet hair,
gave me a notebook and pencil and a paper bag with one round golden biscuit
in it.

He led me to the door of the house and into the street.
I looked up at the mountain and the morning
at the streets full of bloodless dead.

The Cat Has a Mouthful of Larks

The cat has a mouthful of larks
spotted golden fledglings – their wing, song, and the sky unknown to them.
Known only is warm to warm, bird's nest to cat's mouth.
What is to be done?

They lie here stricken with heartbeat.
Not bound to keep an eye
on almost immobility
the cat on the mat, a white goddess,
looks away,
for unadorned place,
concealed time
are not her prey;
only the thing struggling to get, some time (morning, noon, night)
to some place (earth, sky, space).
She will even bring home in her mouth
a travelling beam of light.

What is to be done?
Skylarks are rare these days.
Shelley himself would be forced to practise economy
both of skylark and of simile.
Our poets who go out
in the paddocks don't often chance
on that coincidence of overflowing light and song
directly overhead – or – where?

I said to my mother, Who do you love most.
She said, I love you all. A politician's answer.
Choose then, choose between us,
the lover and the husband said to the lover's mistress
who replied, It's not my place.

How quickly we learn about the goings-on, about loving the least and the most,
how to give words a large coat to fit
neither flea nor giant
how to capture the desirable
how to develop the faculty to torture it.

The Accomplished Snow
(for a friend whose wife died after a long illness)

The death of snow
engages from a whole day to many months.

The death is merely
a change of form
yet how can it know
and why is there no rebellion?

A spectacle of waste
a promise unfulfilled
no anger, only surrender
yet not even surrender

no to and fro struggle
between will of solid and liquid
nothing remarkable at all
or factual, except the recorded time
– a whole day or many months for the snowfall to die.

We want it to be but it is not.
We are cold with the shock, and alone.
Snow is not human. The scene
we gave our unreciprocated wonder to has gone
without agony and will not return.

Eagerly we wait for tomorrow's weather
to share the responsibility of our dying.
We must – to get on with our living – give
pain and splendour to the storm,
simplicity to the rain,
and – hardest of all – the endurance of dying-time
to the accomplished snow.

Two Painters

Two painters, side by side:
one, for whom the body is pencil-strokes of grey ash
broken grey threads too frail for sewing;
strewn eyeless needles whose gleam
like light at the back of the moon plays havoc
with only the few knowing; secret, on the white wall.
A modest man of persistent fire, a prince of light.

There was a man who ordered a case of angels.
They arrived in a box, packed somewhat like apples,
wrapped in layers of cloudy tissue, against decay.
Fearfully he unwrapped them, unfolded their wings,
set them tall in the white room –
what a brilliant array of light cutting a swathe through bed, chair and breakfast
tray
and all the objects of the kingdom.

Two princes of light cutting with their silver knives,
paring the rosy poisoned skin for display
among the pure narcissus of the kingdom.

The heart into canvas.

Words

1

The stain of words will soak through the thickest gloves.
You touch them. They bite and scratch,
your blood mixes with theirs,
changes colour. You never learn
the chemical process of separating them
only stir stir stir
in the crackpot cookpot
dissolving the dear definition.

Arithmetic is always bath-time:
clean, competent, neatly arranging numbers,
no danger from one burdened tower of addition

to its neighbour; no carry-over;
no numb loss in subtraction
fallout from explosive multiplication;
in the face of division
no fear of diminishing possession.

Numbers are a confession
of calculating patterns
a pure telling.
Come clean, God said, You cardinals and ordinals
from the first to the last day.

Hungry among words? Eat between the syllables.
Sleep in two-roomed S
bed upon a hyphen.
A minus sign will not do
having no overlapping involvement
with one and one and two.
In numbers, highways of speed,
the going is good
the subtracted have always been dead.
In words, slow roots of darkness and loss
grow to catch the world in a searchlight
and in the bereaved night the moon
leaning wild with cloud
sweeping up the sea into her face.

2

In Jet flight word games are recommended. Have fun with words:
Puzzles easy medium hard; quizzes; cryptograms;
stung by a spelling bee pluck out the off ending
guttural or plosive, put in a soothing sibilant
as snakes are reputed to do before they strike;
or a ticktocking dental, time on the run.
Words are fun. Try the Biblical quotes:
– Thou shalt love thy neighbour blank thyself.
Seek and blank shall find.
A land flowing with milk and blank.

Wordgames so near heaven, an elemental recreation
playing with fire and air. Sick for earth?
Cure with cuttlefish fluid seven down; three across
dried grass; one down cry of pain;
one across glazed clay square; and so on and on;
large saxhorn, illuminated, scale tone,
nocturnal birds, delicate colour, devoured,

ring metallically, timber wolf, poured,
deep-toned bell;
if ye blank faith as a grain of mustard seed.
Moving at five hundred miles an hour
be comforted to know the soft mineral used for bath powder
the Spanish for gold, a unit of electric force.
Changeling in the air, the sun too close to be mother,
the dark-eyed earth too far, break, break the vowels,
restore lost consonants to stung catastrophes, immortalised colossal
asphyxiation and schism; in the game of changeling
get rice from oats, love from life, bread from death,
take words from compass point,
picnic pests, porcupine's quill and negative reply,
to contend with evergreen, undaunted, you and I,
grow drowsy, tear apart, enclosure for light,
soak as flax, iron-source, pearl-giver, falsehood,
one who throbs with pain, hawthorn, set free,
season of snow and ice, summer flower, sly,
a piece of armour for the head; play,
play at changeling words,
birds that mount singing into heaven, hunter's prey,
– Blessed are the blankmakers
Blank are they that mourn.

3

I swung the axe. I struck.
I decapitated the guilty words.
Neck-high nerve-flinching they
fluttered wildly from the pen. Blood
stuck like a postage-stamp
on the newly addressed earth.
An effort of communication used
only for remotest distance between
person and person.

There remained only
the distasteful ceremony
of eating the words, alone
or in company at a feast;
of cleaning out the once-crowded pen
scrubbing the spattered perch
where they huddled at night
asleep, my feathered friends
their beaks set in the groove
of their wornout 78rpm
Overture to Earliest Light.

It will be quiet without them.
They were so busy
my naked enemies the words
pecking pecking at the earth
and at each other.

If You Don't Wish to Write About People

If you don't wish to write about people, he said,
stick to places, say goodbye to novels,
try writing poems. Poems, you know,
can more easily fit in land and seascapes; a few flowers,
perhaps a garden, a house – many houses to choose from.
Read the real estate pages of your newspaper – view, cannot be built out –
bestone – *be-stone?* – freestanding fire, internal entry,
peep of the sea, ideal first home; established garden, sought-after
neighbourhood; close to schools, shopping centre, churches...
skip the people; no one need live in the house or the street or the
town or the land: make it an empty country.
You see what I mean? poems do well without people.
Turn your love and hate on the sky, the sea, the weather, the trees:
such will suffice.

I mean to say, How can you write a novel without people?
All the he's and she's, the comings and goings, the doings
and thinkings and wonderings, 'the weeping and the laughter, love and desire
and hate'
through the 'postern' – a 'back door, a private door, any door or gate distinct
from the main entrance' – *Oxford Dictionary*. A way of escape or refuge.

An Orange
(a poetry lesson)

Who trapped me in this tangled golden swamp
where breathing juice I struggle
through vine-fibres climbing the pale
oval stones; sweet and it stings; if citrus
suffocation gets me before I make the white padded prison wall
record I died inside an orange drowned in denser
sunlight but neither I nor the news got through.
Why? I'm my own messenger. An ant crying Help Help
on the windowsill has as much hope. Therefore
should I describe the object others might see?

'The globose fruit of the rutaceous tree;
Citrus aurentium; a golden berry.'

Where? I'm still inside the swamp
happily resistant to classical and poetic diseases but
suffocated by Vitamin C.

Daniel

Daniel
who was born manual
who longed to be electric
to go everywhere at the flick
of a switch
met a witch
at the corner of Quinn's Road
where the virgilia tree hangs its palepink sweet-pea flowers.

I've been waiting for you for hours
and years since you were born, Daniel
to show you the trick that will change you
from manual to electric. Watch closely.

Startled into silence, Daniel stared,
his eyes growing round in a circle
instead of eye-shaped.

'There,' the witch said. 'That's the trick. Surprise does it,
and remembering to think or say every hour
and sometimes every minute of every hour, I wonder or I see in my mind's eye
or simply Why, why, why.'

Then the witch of Quinn's Road vanished
among the palepink flowers
of the virgilia tree.

And wink-quick manual Daniel
became Why-electric.

I Write Surrounded by Poets

I write surrounded by poets leaning raggedly, pages missing, on secondhand
                                                                  shelves
from Browns of Dunedin or Interused Furniture of Levin
and between, from the cluttered rooms of Glenfield,
Stratford,
Wanganui,
shelves lying once beside boxes of bonehandled knives and silver forks from
                                                                  Sheffield.
I write with the secondhand stink in my nose
an old stink of the leftovers of death
hammered, nailed wood treated, dressed,
tablecloths with their heavenly image
grey tableforks standing with legs twisted in a garden plot.

And what of the poets and the slim books with space to spare on each page,
the words arranged each alone speaking for itself, living or dying by its shape
or place of whirl, coil, spring of meaning?

The sweet daily bread of language.
Smell it rising in its given warmth
taste it through the stink of tears and yesterdays and
eat it anywhere with any angel in sight.

Some of My Friends Are Excellent Poets

Some of my friends are excellent poets
modestly packed with knowhow, the practising a craft look about them
in control of their words which in print
are welldressed in the classical style.
Even were they barefoot, in rags, they would have dignity
I tell you, some of my friends are excellent poets.

I survey a rough land. I have no theodolite.
I'm a foreign settler.
I haven't paid for my acres.
I don't know how to crop them.
Why am I so obstinately trying to write poetry?

It's a habit. In all the years I've been alive
habits have been classified as good or bad.
Bad habits bring ruination (a fine word, a poem in itself).
Writing poetry is not a bad habit
though the poems may turn out to be habitually bad
with the thoughts habitually thought
the words in their habitual place.

Poetry has not room for timidity of tread
tiptoeing in foot prints already made
running afraid of the word-stranger glimpsed out of the corner of the eye
lurking in the wilderness. Poetry is a time for the breaking of habits good or bad,
a breaking free of memory and yesterday
to face the haunting that is.

You see? What have we been? We are nothing to a poem.
We have no possession of pronoun. We start with nothing
but pain that does not exist and worm-words eating at the arm.
Not even that.
This is my life and it is my habit
said the poet.

The Cat of Habit

The cat of habit
knows the place by heart
or at least by space, scent, direction, bulk,
by shadow and light
moonlight starlight sunlight
and where to nest in each
with a three-focussed shut eye
on who or what's coming and going
on the earth and in the sky
and distantly, not present, the rays of inkling
shining within the furred skull.

The cat of habit curls her spine
in the most windless the most warm place
shivering a little with, 'It's mine',
an ear-twitch, tail-flip
of permanent ownership.

The cat of habit
has the place marked,
the joint cased.

Feed and sleep and feed
and half-heartedly catch
moths and mice and mostly watch
hourlong for the passing witch
for many, unseen, pass
through the rooms of the house and outside,
under the trees and in the grass.

Swatting Flies

Flies are awake bodies and mouths.
I have written the first draught of my novel.

Immeasurable dullness
of the mind at work under the heavy mosscovered stone
or under the sky's wide blue wing

or the green-needled boughs growing
up through sleep
the darting stinging reproducing flies copper-burnished
glass-green homing
without foreknowledge or memory
to where the dark woods and their beasts
weathered, lived by my life, decay
and decaying offer the imaginative feast
to flies honey-combing the silence with noisy sparkle.

In my dullness I take this black velvet-bordered flyswat,
the only wickedness in my pure studio, something symbolic
no doubt, and swat them hard. Squash. They split.
The ideas come out unformed; hideous to see
– also to contemplate their being the unborn larvae
nourished at the feast of me.

On another day
with clearer head
after I have faced the fact that the first draught of my novel must be read
I will let the flies be and fly until they are dead
and over the white page see
what they have laid
full-term ideas formed by my deepest layers of decay
while I in my dullness
resting motionless in silence
will remember that the view and the passion are best caught
when face and heart but not necessarily fly-swat
are turned away.

A New Cheese

My book has gone sour.
Its acid bacteria have multiplied
in the heat of my effort.
It stands with a thick skin on top,
curdled. The best I can hope for
is to leave it, let it ripen, mature
to a cheese of sharp taste and foul odour.

Poets

If poets die young
they bequeath two thirds of their life to the critics
to graze and grow fat in
visionary grass.

If poets die in old age
they live their own lives
they write their own poems
they are their own might-have-been.

Young dead poets are prized comets.
The critics queue with their empty wagons ready for hitching.

Old living poets
stay faithfully camouflaged in their own sky.
It may even be forgotten they have been shining for so long.
The reminder comes upon their falling
extinguished into the earth.
The sky is empty, the sun and moon have gone away,
there are not enough street bulbs, glow-worms, fireflies to give light

and for a time it seems there will be no more stars.

7

Appearing

Letters in my morning mail keep asking me,
'We would like you to appear... Will you appear?'

I, the disappeared, la disparue, the invisible,
remembering the childhood serial
of the man who pressed his navel or belly button
to go back and forth from visible to invisible,
wonder do I, too, have some such accomplishment
I'm not aware of.

'We would like you to appear...'

As bellybuttons are too eternally a-fashioned,
I press Run/Stop Restore, CTRL, or Shift
or choosing my colour, enter rainbows, Return.
The magic is dubious. To all appearances, though
I'm quite visible; therefore
there's no need to appear.

Thank you for your kind invitation.
I'm already visible
if in a peculiar way out of your view.

Small Farewell

Writing letters of goodbye
we are inclined to say
because we have read
or heard it said
or knew someone who likewise went away
that small details pester the memory.

In the corner closet of your eye
in the back room of seeing
that looks out on the backyard of yesterday
who can pretend to say
what you will muffle in moth balls
or soak with insect spray
to stop the spread of memory's decay?

I think all I can say
from hearing a ghost speak in a Shakespeare play
is, if you were Hamlet, and I your father's ghost,
– Remember me.

The Old Bull

On the edge of town
in a paddock summer brown
the old bull stands alone
watching the cars whiz by
with their coats shining, their horns
honking silly tunes, their eyes intense, glaring,
part of a brightly coloured herd roaming
freely to everywhere and anywhere at faster speed
than ever the old bull had.

The old bull drinks at the rusted watertank.
He blinks his bloodshot eyes.
He swishes his tail at the blowflies.
He grunts, snorts, watches a while
the young herd of bullocks
futureless in the paddocks
on the edge of town
near the brick units and the new Rest Home.

Neither happy nor sad
the old bull just being and standing
like a piece of used furniture
old oak ready to whiten in the sun
old oak, old bull
pride of the farm
of the farmer who grew old
who said, I'll subdivide
the farm on the edge of town
and the old bull and I will stand side by side,
he in his paddock
I in my unit of brick
watching the herd of traffic.

The Dead

The dead have worn out my grief.
I gave it to them to wear
renewing it year after year
nor was I the sole supplier.

When was it they returned, complaining?
Was it at Christmas or one St Agnes Eve
(they having once read Keats
and suffered the doubly inspired chill)
claiming the clothing of tears had dried
to a grassgreen universal shroud
and after their pampering by individual fashion
in private salons lined with satin
some contract they declare they never signed
decreed it time for them to share
the wide world? At first resentful, reluctant
they tried to keep warm by wearing
the shadow of their past personal pronoun
but it wouldn't fit: they had outgrown it
into vastness.
               I smile to see them now,
how contentedly they are clothed with sun!

The Recent Dead

Seen through the mirror
in a lilac tree in an unnamed garden
two sparrows in love breast a wave of summer,
dipping, kissing, tipsy a little,
drinking a thimbleful of breath
of lilac, of rhododendron,
of dark exhaust of oil, burning and blood
swept from the turning midnight of the geophysical year.

Seen through the mirror a terrible blossom-white fungus
is nursed in a blue cellar of sky.
Master of the house upstairs,
Are you the sun, the fire, or simply my father slumped asleep in the heat
on a terrace rococo with angels?

Are you at home or have you never bought up all that emptiness
for sale in us, all our darkening acres of sky?
Or were you hung for plain speaking on a mountain,
on a day of too much love in too many mirrors,
while Death, athletic in the summer world,
Death clerical, obliging, kept a note of sparrows falling
out of the lilac and the flushed rhododendron?

Friends Far Away Die

Friends far away die
friends measured always in blocks of distance
cement of love between
porous to tears and ocean spray
how vast the Pacific!
How heavy the unmiracled distance to walk upon,
a slowly sinking dream, a memory undersea.
Untouched now, Sue, by storm
easy to reach
an angel-moment away,
hostess of memories in your long green gown, your small blue
slippers lying on the white sofa
in the room I once knew – the tall plants behind you –
I remember I watered them and found some were fake
and I shrugged, thinking it's part of life

to feed the falseness, the artificial, but no, you fed only truth
you cut down every growing pretence with one cool glance.
We were at home with you.
We knew, as people say, where we stood.
Your beloved John of the real skin and uncopied eyes was anxious for you
in true anxiety.

Well, you will visit me in moments.
You will be perplexed yet wise, as usual.
Perhaps we will drink won ton soup.
I promise you. No food will hurt you now.

It All Happened; It Was Yesterday

At night when I stared too hard at the trunks of the coconut palms
they moved like crocodiles.
Their leaves were rattlesnakes.
The dark sang in my ears like the sea.
The woodpeckers pecked my eyes into flute-holes.

It all happened; it was yesterday.

Yesterday, move a little to the right, into focus.
Tomorrow, come forward.
But do not smile, do not say cheese.
Only weep weep without teeth or gums, with a cry
like a marsh bird alone in the marsh
with the tides of mist and loneliness rising.

Stung by Ideas

Stung by ideas we danced in pain
until Time came
with the forceps used on Birthdays
and drew the sting from our head.
You may sleep now, he said, and never fear another swarm;
forgetting that from pear-tree to pear-tree
the invisible bees must go
with handbags of harm like love-letters
and hate-forecasts of snow
under the risible slapstick sun
where all scream or fall down
praying or dead,
and the only comic film
is old age clouding the eyes
and a swarm of hiveless bees in the head.

The Magazine

My mother used to say, Beware of the Magazine!
She said it was used in wartime to kill.
Dynamite. A deadly explosive.
Kept in a shed behind the old railway-yellow drill-hall
where the returned soldiers stood at ease, presented arms and marched to
                                                              Colonel Bogey.
Bare wooden floor, stacked seats assembled for Sunday school,
a prize giving, an Agricultural and Pastoral show
with the Governor General, marble in mouth, medal on chest, moustache on lip,
zealously praising the nation
and the children waiting near for the teacher to signal, A hearty hip-hip-hip!
Rows and rows of scones on plates,
cream sponges and puffs, pikelets, bouquets, butterfat,
tractors, the story of wool
from sheep to the coat on a woman's back.
Statistics, beheaded people, and people with half-bodies and minds.
(My country 'twas always of thee
thou sheeply haven for the insomniac!
We learned to wear you nearest our skin to keep us warm.
You were natural, not manmade; you breathed but by God
you itched
and everyone was too polite to scratch!)

Meanwhile
in the small shed behind the drill-hall
the deadly *magazine* waited its chance – Oh my! Its explosion blew
the marble from the Governor General's mouth,
the trim moustache from his lip,
melted his medals at whiter than white heat.

Now tourists come to see the shadow butter,
the plates of scones burned into the landscape,
tall stick people with half bodies and minds.

This way for the world's only durable atomic shadow
of a woman's virgin wool cardigan and winter coat!
This way for the only sound shadow of school-children cheering a hearty
                                                              hip-hip-hip!
For the world's only military moustache blown from a Governor General's lip!

But all that was long ago now. Alpha and Omega,
the beginning and the end.

What I Have Seen or Dreamed

What have I seen or dreamed?
I have seen an owl polishing its glass eye,
Aldebaran, Betelgeuse,
A mouse sitting at a small sewing-machine
making trapdoor covers for the President's memory,
a spoon at the beginning of its tether
of submissive behaviour,
articles not human remaining not human
slipping each time from the anthropomorphological harness.
Indian beads on a gold chain.
A Highway notice reading *To Blame*.
The inhabitants of Blame reciting their diet sheet in the public square.

I have seen what is not acknowledged to be there
like double-headed people with double heads of hair
and presumably double brains (to be fair)
triple sandstorms rising in the Frigidaire,
Thursday unable to be preserved, turning sour.

I have seen Euclid bare and was interested
how purely congruent were his triangles
how right his rhombus
no other theorem could have been so beautifully binomial.

Joking and fantasy apart, and all in all,
the principal thing seen and dreamed is Death.

The End

At the end
I have to move my sight up or down.
The path stops here.
Up is heaven, down is ocean
or, more simply, sky and sea rivalling
in welcome, crying Fly (or Drown) in me.
I have always found it hard to resist an invitation
especially when I have come to a dead end
a
dead
end.

The trees that grow along cliff-faces,
having suffered much from weather, put out thorns
taste of salt
ignore leaf-perm and polish:
hags under matted white hair
parcels of salt with the string tangled;
underneath
thumping the earth with their rebellious root-foot
trying to knock up
peace
out of her deep sleep.

I suppose, here, at the end, if I put out a path upon the air
I could walk on it, continue my life;
a plastic carpet, tight-rope style
but I've nothing beyond the end to hitch it to,
I can't see into the mist across the ocean;
I shall have to change to a bird or a fish.

I can't camp here at the end.
I wouldn't survive
unless returning to a mythical time
I became a tree
toothless with my eyes full of salt spray;
rooted, protesting on the edge of this cliff
– Let me stay!

The Turquoise Bird

In fairy tales death
always invites the blossoming of a flower or bird
the creation of a beautiful creature
who stays in the same place forever
and is disconcerting to the world
because it stays and does nothing but be what it is
and stare down surrounded by light
upon the darkness of what it used to be.

The turquoise bird stares into the grave.

How I Began Writing

1

Between myself and the pine trees on the hill
Thoughts passed, like presents. Unwrapping them, I found
words that I, not trees, knew and could afford:
lonely, sigh, night. The pines had given me
my seven-year self, but kept their own meaning in the sky.

Now, in exchange of dreams with this remote world
I still unwrap, identify the presents;
and always tired recognition gives way to hope
that soon I may find a new, a birthday shape,
a separate essence yielded without threat or deceit,
a truthful vocabulary of what is and is not.

2

Vowels turn like wheels: the chariot is empty.
Tall burning consonants light the deserted street.
Unwrapping the world,
unwrapping the world
where pine trees still say lonely, sigh, night, and refuse,
refuse, and their needles of deceit drop in my eyes,
I began to write.

AFTERWORD

Janet spent her final years in Dunedin, and Pamela and I went for many a 'spin' with her to the shops, to do errands, or (her favourite) to do lunch. Though Janet would not talk about what she was writing, sometimes she would be excited about it, and say she was keen to get back to work. She often quoted snatches of poetry to counterpoint talk of friends, politics and weather, and I would try to guess the poet – usually one of the greats she remembered from old school anthologies such as *Mount Helicon*. Once, when we parked beside the Admiral Byrd Memorial overlooking the harbour, we were stumped by her recital of a verse about Antarctica that ended with the couplet:

> Oates, Evans, Bowers, Wilson and Scott,
> By the world forgotten not.

That final rhyme made us all hoot with delight. We were unable to guess the author, so slyly she told us: 'It was...me.' Even though she was now laughing at herself, she said that verse had been one of the triumphs of her schooldays.

After Janet's death it was my job to burrow through her hoard of poetry manuscripts stacked in various rooms. There were thousands of sheets of paper in dozens of manila folders in and around the ubiquitous white file-boxes containing the rest of her documents. Janet bequeathed her literary papers to the Hocken Library, but she made an exception for her unpublished work, which was to remain with her estate. One of the boxes that did find its way to the Hocken had been her elderly cat Penny's favourite sleeping place, located near a sunny window in the back study. Janet had written 'Penny's Box' on this one, and it presented the archivists with a cataloguing puzzle for it included Penny's hairbrush and a small can of gourmet cat-food. Looking through the folders I found some splendid cat poems, such as 'The Cat of Habit', in which Janet observes that a cat will always choose 'the most windless the most warm place'.

Most pages were typed, with some revised by hand. There were very few handwritten texts. I made copies of the manuscripts, pre-serving their arrangement, but it soon became clear there was no obvious order. The original typescripts were on many kinds and colours of paper (green, yellow, pink, blue and white) with a number of different typefaces. The collection also included numerous faded carbon copies. There was considerable evidence of shuffling, of re-sorting. Many of the older pages were crumpled and dog-eared; some looked like they had been screwed up at one stage. There were multiple photocopies of almost everything, as Janet had owned her own photocopiers and used them extensively. To complicate matters, she had often revised and re-numbered the duplicate pages as well as the originals. In-depth study will be needed to establish the chronology and relationships of these drafts. Investigation of the numbering systems (some sheets have three different page numbers) will yield valuable clues. Janet made about ten different lists of poems over the years, indicating repeated attempts to form a collection.

Further research is also needed to establish the relationship of her poetry to her prose. Occasionally, one format has been transformed into the other. For example 'Worms' is a poem, but also appears as prose in her unpublished 1963 novella *Towards Another Summer*. 'The Servant' also exists in both verse and prose variants. Janet referred to this mutability:

> I have always thought there was something magical about writing, and how it can be changed, buried, resurrected, influenced, and even added to by others with their own point of view. Very often a poem becomes a story or a novel, or a story becomes a novel.
> [*undated manuscript notes for an interview*]

In other cases, a poem is either put into or taken out of a prose context. For instance, Janet inserted a poem into *Living in the Maniototo* that she later recorded for the Poetry Archive under the title 'The Scarlet Tanager'. 'Nails as a Rose' has been lifted out of a surrounding prose passage. Further poems employing concepts like 'manifold' or 'gravity star' clearly relate to certain of her novels. Because of these transformations we have to expect that some poems in *The Goose Bath* may well have left traces in other places.

Almost all the manuscripts are undated, but internal and external references have enabled us to date some poems approximately. The earliest verifiable date for a poem in *The Goose Bath* is 1958 for 'A Specimen in the Maudsley Brain Museum'. Some other poems in *The Goose Bath* have also appeared in print. Details of their first publication, where known, are to be found in the notes that end this book. We acknowledge that our information is incomplete. There is as yet no definitive bibliography of Janet Frame's individually published poems, especially the occasional and political verse printed in newspapers, and poems published during her time spent overseas.

We did not consider any of her published juvenilia for this volume, and neither have we selected any of the poems that appeared in the early 1950s in the *New Zealand Listener* and *Landfall*. With one or two exceptions, she seems not to have kept her own copies of those poems. We are not certain how much of her early unpublished poetry survives, as in 1956 she burnt a manuscript of poems that Denis Glover of Caxton Press had returned to her. She told Glover she was 'burying the ashes in the garden as nourishment for the sweet corn', and the poem 'Sweet Corn' appears to refer to that deed.

By the time Janet published her sole book of poetry *The Pocket Mirror* in 1967, she had accumulated 300 poems (according to a letter to her American publisher George Braziller). Most of the 160 printed in that volume were written in just two years, between 1964 and 1966 in Dunedin. We found some poems from *The Pocket Mirror* half buried in *The Goose Bath*. They were hard to spot due to Janet's habit of changing titles and adding or deleting words and stanzas. 'Blame the Tokarahis' and 'Why I Began Writing' are two examples of this reworking that we decided to retain because they are sufficiently different from the original poems, and they give a good insight into her craft.

We have so far identified at least 500 unpublished poems. This number continues to grow as further poems turn up from other sources. Every foray into the Hocken archive unearths more gems, and the investigating and cataloguing of the Janet Frame papers has barely begun. We are also tracking down poems that are held privately in collections of Janet's correspondence or in other repositories in New Zealand and elsewhere. In the preliminary selection for this book, we chose around 250 poems, which I transcribed. The key editorial policy for *The Goose Bath* was to tamper as little as possible with Janet's work, so we chose only finished poems. We therefore had to forego many brilliant fragmentary or unpolished pieces which may well appear in the future in a suitably edited edition.

After selection, the next task was to arrange the poems. Whatever arrangement we chose would be arbitrary, in light of the death of the author. The conventional sequence for a posthumous publication is chronological, but a detailed timeline is not possible at this early stage of research. As I became familiar with the poems they clustered round many of Janet's favourite themes such as time, seasons, snow, cats, words, death, etc. I tentatively assembled these themes into two overriding categories: those concerned with the natural world and those concerned with the human world, both often tending towards a third category, best represented in fable and dream. This working model had resonances with Lawrence Jones's overview of the world created in Janet Frame's published works:

> It is a world consisting of three realms that impinge on individual lives: the realm of Nature, Time and Death; that of Society; and that of the 'Mirror City' of the individual inner life.
> [Introduction, *The Carpathians*, 2005]

This initial selection and arrangement was still too large and unwieldy. There was a superfluity of poems on similar themes, and some of the multiple variants of poems had been reworked into and out of longer sequences, so that phrases and passages recurred in different places. At this point we turned to Bill Manhire to apply his discerning eye. With fine judgement and a sharp scalpel, he pared the selection to half its size again and conceived of a narr-ative structure that would locate the poems along a path roughly following Janet's own journey in life. Once this biographical traj-ectory was agreed upon it became surprisingly easy for us to decide on the choice of poems, debate their order, and work out which variant to favour.

I have been privileged to conduct a first archaeological dig into the trove of Janet's poems, all of which we expect will eventually find a home in a Collected edition. Her poetry evolved from an early rhetorical and somewhat derivative style influenced by the likes of Gerard Manley Hopkins, Dylan Thomas and George Barker (a style represented only minimally in *The Goose Bath*) to a clarity and simplicity (abundant in *The Pocket Mirror*) that by the 1990s fully conveyed her unique voice.

DENIS HAROLD

NOTES

Worms (33)
A prose version of this poem appears in JF's posthumously published novel *Towards Another Summer* (written in 1963).

A Simple Memory of a Poet, a Memory Shuffled Face Upward (34)
What we have assumed to be the title is handwritten at the top of the page (this poem is heavily revised by hand). Mary Ellen Blair (1875–1963) of Gisborne wrote a book of verse, *Kowhai Blossoms*, in 1929.

For Paul on His Birthday (35)
This poem is addressed to Janet's friend Paul Wonner. The poem shares some features with the poem written for her friend Bill Brown. In the first line, 'We were the railway children' alludes to Edith Nesbit's classic children's novel *The Railway Children* (1906). The quotation is from the sequence *Vergers* (Orchards), written in French by the German poet Rainer Maria Rilke. An appropriate English translation is 'Stay calm, if the angel suddenly chooses your table'.

The Happy Prince (36)
The children of JF's sister June Gordon had a book-and-record version of Oscar Wilde's story *The Happy Prince*. This poem was published in the *New Zealand Listener*, August 28, 2004.

I Visited (37)
This appears as a section in a long untitled sequence.

The Tom Cat Which Sargeson Refused to Have Neutered (42)
This poem refers to Frank Sargeson, JF's mentor and friend. JF has handwritten across the top of the page: 'Finally, <u>The Tom Cat</u> unchanged, entire, <u>which Sargeson refused to have neutered</u>, alter.' We have chosen to interpret the underlined portion as the title, the rest perhaps as preparatory comments for a reading.

To FS Who Shaved His Beard (42)
FS is Frank Sargeson.

A Visitor to Cornwall (44)
In March 1962, JF spent a fortnight at the Cornish town of Mevagissey, in a seaside cottage belonging to her literary agent Patience Ross. This poem almost certainly arises from that experience.

The Icicles (46)
A recording of JF reading this poem in 2002 is lodged with the Aotearoa New Zealand Poetry Sound Archive.

A Specimen in the Maudsley Brain Museum (49)
Written while JF was cataloguing medical papers in the brain museum of the Royal Maudsley Hospital, London, early in 1958. This version differs slightly from the one printed in Chapter 15 of *The Envoy from Mirror City* (the third volume of her autobiography), in which she substitutes 'Dobson's tumour' for 'Parker's tumour'.

The Servant (49)
There is also a prose version of this poem.

Nails as a Rose (51)
This poem was found as a single page among JF's poems. It was also found later among her other papers, in a prose context.

A Field of Wheat (52)
There is a prose version of this poem.

Norfolk Evening (54)
This poem also appears as part four of a longer unpublished poem entitled 'Norfolk Verse'. JF's friend Peter (Elizabeth) Dawson lived in Norfolk, and later bequeathed her Norfolk cottage to JF.

The Advice of Light (56)
In her later years JF is known to have regretted her early use of the generic 'man' in this poem and others; like most writers she discarded the usage once it was recognised as unconsciously sexist. She felt that the archaism 'dated' those poems.

Blame the Tokarahis (56)
The Tokarahis and Kakanuis are ranges of hills inland from Oamaru. Some lines in the last stanza were published in *The Pocket Mirror* as 'Return' [not included in the Bloodaxe selection].

Sweet Corn (57)
This poem seems to refer to a 1956 incident when JF burned a poetry manuscript that Denis Glover of Caxton Press had returned to her. JF wrote to Glover that she was 'burying the ashes in the garden as nourishment for the sweet corn'.

The Leech (58)
The Leech-gatherer is a character in Wordsworth's poem 'Resolution and Independence'.

And the Sound of the Cellos (59)
This poem also appears as a part of a long sequence.

Drought in Another Country (64)
JF often visited her friends in Berkeley, California. A recording of JF reading this poem in 2002 is lodged with the Aotearoa New Zealand Poetry Sound Archive.

The Guggenheim Museum, New York (65)
This museum is shaped like a giant spiral nautilus shell.

An Exhibit in the Pre-Columbian Room, Dumbarton Oaks Museum, Washington (65)
Published on 2 January 2000, in a *Sunday Star-Times* special edition celebrating the new millennium.

Saratoga Walk (66)
JF stayed a number of times at Yaddo, the artists' community in Saratoga Springs, upstate New York. 'Modess' was a female sanitary product.

For Bill on His Birthday (69)
Addressed to her piano-playing friend Bill (William Theophilus) Brown, the Californian painter she met in 1969 when she stayed at MacDowell, the artists' colony in New Hampshire. The Rilke quotation, included in both poems, also inspired the title of her second volume of autobiography, *An Angel at My Table*.

In Mexico City (70)
In the course of her travels, JF made occasional short stop-overs in Mexico. On her first visit she suffered altitude sickness, which may account for the 'suffering' of the tourist in this poem. An almost identical version was published in the *New Zealand Listener*, 20 December 1968.

Baltimore, November (71)
JF's friend and mentor, the sexologist Dr John Money, lived in a seedy part of Baltimore city, near Johns Hopkins University. JF stayed at his home many times between 1964 and 2001.

The Legend (72)
One of many 'New Hampshire poems' arising from JF's stay at the MacDowell artists' colony.

Martha's Vineyard (74)
The New England island is noted for its whaling history, and the 'white whale' refers to *Moby Dick* by Herman Melville. JF spent a

weekend there with the Marquand family in the summer of 1967. 'Martha's Vineyard' is the typed title of the poem. JF has handwritten 'A State of Summer' and 'A Souvenir' at the top of the page; these may refer to plans for a longer work, as 'The State of Summer' also appears as one of several sub-headings she has written in an exercise book. The other sub-headings (such as 'Joyful Change') are also found handwritten above some of JF's poems.

A Pearl of Oblivion (77)
One of the New Hampshire poems. An alternative title JF offered for this piece is 'Something Dead'.

Calypso (79)
There are several variants of this poem, both as a stand-alone and as part of a longer sequence, 'Salt Cay', which is based on JF's holiday with the Marquand family on a private island in the Bahamas.

Letter from Lake Bomoseen (79)
Addressed to JF's dying friend Frank Sargeson. Persil was the resident cat at North Shore Hospital, Auckland, where JF had visited Sargeson. The poem was written in 1982 at Lake Bomoseen (which JF misspelt as 'Bomaseen'), Vermont. FS died some weeks later, before she could send it to him. It was first published in *An Affair of the Heart: A Celebration of Frank Sargeson's Centenary*, edited by Graeme Lay and Stephen Stratford (Auckland: Cape Catley, 2003).

Eater of Crayfish (87)
Published in the *New Zealand Listener*, 28 August 2004.

The Landfall Desk (91)
In 1966, when Charles Brasch retired from editing the New Zealand literary journal *Landfall*, he gave JF the journal's desk. It accompanied her as far as Levin and now resides at the International Institute of Modern Letters at Victoria University, Wellington. This poem was set by hand and printed by Brendan O'Brien at Wai te-ata Press, Wellington, in 2002. A text of the poem also appears on the institute's website at http://www.vuw.ac.nz/modernletters/framepoem.html.

Words Speak to Jakow Trachtenberg (96)
Trachtenberg (1888–1953) was born in Russia and moved to Germany after the 1917 revolution. To survive as a political prisoner in a Nazi concentration camp, he occupied his mind with developing techniques in speed mathematics. After escaping to Switzerland, he founded an institute in Zurich where he taught his system. JF had a great love for mathematics.

Talk of Economy (100)
'Sulphothion' most likely refers to or is intended to suggest a controversial agricultural chemical, perhaps an organo-phosphate.

If I Read St John of the Cross (101)
JF wrote this poem during her period in Stratford (1976–79) when she was 'taking instruction' at the local Catholic church. St John of the Cross was a sixteenth-century Spanish priest who wrote mystical verse.

On December 31st Each Year (103)
The references to Wanganui strongly suggest that this poem was written between 1979 and 1983, the period JF lived there. It was her habit to reread Pepys's diaries at the beginning of each year. Frank Sargeson was probably one of the recently dead writers to whom she refers.

Pictures Never Painted, Music Never Composed (104)
One of many poems written after the death of her cat, Neggy (named 'Negative' because she was a white cat). Neggy died in November 1986.

Lines Written at the Frank Sargeson Centre (108)
This poem dates from early 1987 when JF was the first Sargeson Fellow, based in the studio of the Sargeson Centre next to Albert Park in Auckland. The Euganean Hills refer to Shelley's poem 'Lines Written from the Euganean Hills'. *The Aspern Papers* is a story by Henry James; Nathaniel Hawthorne was a nineteenth-century American novelist and short-story writer; Philidor's Defence is a chess strategy well known to serious players. A recording of JF reading this poem in 2002 is lodged with the Aotearoa New Zealand Poetry Sound Archive.

The Accomplished Snow (116)
The note 'written for a friend whose wife died after a long illness' appears on an early draft.

Two Painters (117)
The painters are Janet's friends Bill Brown and Paul Wonner, of California.

Words (117)
Part 2 was published as 'Jet Flight' in the *New Zealand Listener*, 8 August 1969.

Daniel (121)
JF's great-nephew (Pamela Gordon's son) Daniel Bailey was eight

years old in 1985 when this poem was written. Quinn's Road is in Levin. A recording of JF reading this poem in 2002 is lodged with the Aotearoa New Zealand Poetry Sound Archive. The recording was played at the Going West Festival in 2004.

The Cat of Habit (124)

A recording of JF reading this poem in 2002 is lodged with the Aotearoa New Zealand Poetry Sound Archive. This was played (with her prior permission) at JF's private funeral, 31 January 2004.

The Old Bull (129)

A recording of JF reading this poem in 2002 is lodged with the Aotearoa New Zealand Poetry Sound Archive.

Friends Far Away Die (131)

'Sue' is New Yorker Sue Marquand: Janet's close friend, who died in January 1977 of throat cancer. A recording of JF reading this poem in 2002 is lodged with the Aotearoa New Zealand Poetry Sound Archive. It was played at JF's public memorial service in the Dunedin Town Hall on 14 February 2004. The reading is also archived online at the New Zealand Electronic Poetry Centre: *www: nzepc@auckland.ac.nz.*

The Magazine (133)

An arms storage facility such as the one described in this poem was located near the Oamaru foreshore, close to JF's childhood home.

What I Have Seen or Dreamed (134)

Aldebaran and Betelgeuse are stars; Euclid was an ancient Greek mathematician.

The End (134)

Published in the *New Zealand Listener*, 28 August 2004.

How I Began Writing (137)

A variant of the first two stanzas appeared in *The Pocket Mirror* under the first-line title 'Once, Between Myself and the Pine Trees' [not included in the Bloodaxe selection].

ACKNOWLEDGEMENTS

The editors would like to thank all those who made this book possible, and who helped in its production.

We would first of all like to acknowledge the late Michael King for his painstaking workmanship in writing *Wrestling with the Angel: A Life of Janet Frame*. The biography has been indispensible in our research; we are grateful to Michael for that, and for so much else.

Next, we warmly thank Lawrence Jones for his wise advice and generous support for this project in his role as a member of the Board of the Janet Frame Literary Trust.

We have received considerable assistance from the English Department of the University of Otago, including a research grant for Denis Harold; we thank the expert team at Random House New Zealand for their patience and enthusiasm; we have appreciated the use of the facilities and the helpfulness of the staff of the Hocken Library and the Alexander Turnbull Library; thanks are also due to the International Institute of Modern Letters at Victoria University.

We are also grateful for the support and encouragement given by many individuals, including (but not limited to) the following: Chris Ackerley, Harriet Allan, Elizabeth Alley, Jacquie Baxter, Tom Beran, Anna Blackman, Jacob Edmond, June and Wilson Gordon, Claire Gummer, John Irwin, Jan Kemp, Owen Marshall, Richard Reeve, Karl Stead, Stuart Strachan, Lyn Tribble and Lydia Wevers.

PAMELA GORDON
DENIS HAROLD
BILL MANHIRE

THE POCKET MIRROR
(1967)

Dunedin Poem

Here I've gone down with the sun
written syllables till time has surprised me
with the fact of his consistency.
I love not you but the sun's going down
so easily.

Soon will the days be dark? Will the mists come,
the rain blow from Signal Hill down North East Valley
that in winter lies in shadow?
I never remember the sun, in North East Valley.

The tramlines are torn from their sockets.
Things do not suffer as we supposed.
People suffer more than we supposed.
The buses tread softly, jerk to a stop, the doors slide open.
I climb in, travelling to where
down a long street lined with flowering cherry trees I walked
nineteen years ago
to stare at the waves on St Clair beach.

The Clock Tower

I have settled now in my flat.
I have arranged my favourite books on the bookshelf.
I have moved the table for working in privacy and light.

There's a ripe grape-coloured cherry tree,
a bed of geraniums,
a woman walking in white shoes, white gloves, white hat.

A seagull circles the clock tower. His funereal white wings recall
pieces of old tombstone flying
when the wind strikes at the grave of a sea city.

Fog clouds drift on the hill.
Who lives, like an angel, in the clock tower?
The summer heat treads the colour from the cherry tree.

The gracious cultural burden of the View,
the long-faced clean houses that claim their natural right
to hold students, books, to have high ceilings, white walls, neat flower beds,
will soon, I think, send my journeying memory into collapse.
Tomorrow I may be saying, There are no slums in St Kilda.
Hillside Road, the Workshops, Kensington are dreams.
I never lived in Playfair Street, Caversham, with my bedroom a linen cupboard,
or waited on a Saturday night party at the Grand Hotel,
or tried to resist the pleas of my hangwomen workmates.
                          – You
need pearls.
Pearls take away that bare look from the neck.

Swans whose necks are bare
float on the Water of Leith.
The wind is south.
The century is late.

Six o'clock wine flows from the cherry tree.
Children go barefoot,
men and women make promises.
None know, few care
who lives, like an angel, in the clock tower.

Sunday Afternoon at Two O'Clock

Downstairs a sweeping broom goes knock-knock-knock
in the corners getting rid of last week's dust.
The weather hasn't decided to rain or shine.
Downstairs the washing is hung out, brought in, hung out again on the clothesline.

Having been to church the people are good, quiet,
with sober drops at the end of their cold Dunedin noses,
with polite old-fashioned sentences like Pass the Cruet,
and, later, attentive glorying in each other's roses.

The wind combs the seagulls, like dandruff, out of the sky.
They settle, flaked small, on stone shoulder and steeple,
a city coastal infection without remedy.
Their scattered sea-hungry flocks disturb the good people.

Long past is Sunday dinner and its begpardons.
Cars start in the street. The ice-cream shop is open.
The brass band gets ready to play in the Botanical Gardens.
The beach, the pictures, the stock-car racing tracks beckon.

Seizing the time from the University clock, the wind
suddenly cannot carry its burden of chiming sound.
The waves ride in, tumultuous, breaking gustily out of tune,
burying
          two o'clock on Sunday afternoon.

I Must Go Down to the Seas Again

I must go down to the seas again
to find where I
buried the hatchet with Yesterday.

Big Bill

Big Bill, Big Bill, High School Boy, Accountant,
Cricket star, hero of Plunket Shield play,
thirteen years ago I went to your wedding
at St Kilda on a cold dark winter's day.

What happened between then and now, Big Bill,
to bring madness, murder, suicide your way,
riding with us in triple nightmare to your funeral
at St Kilda on this cold dark winter's day?

'It was all over so soon in the neat suburban street
with the faded flowers in the garden.
The time of firing, the number of shots, the angle of the bullets
are not relevant for long,
but love and dread are: love and dread stay.
Others may have the pleasure and curse of them now; not I.
No one will want to own me or bury me. Much wrangling,
cross-questioning, witnessing, will wear the time away
as I go in triple nightmare to my funeral
at St Kilda on this cold dark winter's day.'

Dunedin Morning

The Leith is always a loud grumbler
after a feed of high-country rain
and cannot keep its wide apron clean.

Smoke is early, earliest.
Birds wake, test gear, rest,
make a more subdued start upmorning.

On the city's doorstep, light,
diluted with last night's rain,
is taken in, opened, and seen

to be morning below the usual level of sun.
Cars, motorcycles, people start to complain.
Wise Swampy wears well-bred coney on her shoulder.

Down comes the rain; and later,
in the city of the Globe, the Playhouse and His Majesty's Theatre,
with an expert change of scene, the noon sun.

Leith Street

From black-edged matchbox buds
the elms have shaken out
their silk handkerchief leaves
promising fire later; green
waving streamers glossy ribbons,
what do they mean why must they mean,
we'll not go satisfied
unless there is explaining:
at ear-level the gift is pearl-drop;
to be and mean and stand in spring leaf
is triply possible; sun
brushes a leaf; what gilt; what guilt
turns the spring highway to stone;
as out of the wax vestas the melting virgins come
blossom and burn; oh no,
this is an innocent birthday party where magicians
dazzle with silk handkerchiefs and snow,
think rabbits, live their habits
but never know, never know.

156

Chant

Down with summer spring autumn winter
give me deep freeze for ever
icicles on roofs walls windows the allwhite
alltime allover dream of a world and its people frozen
within the blackest night, so black it's impossible to discern
the alltime allover allwhite dream.

Now blind eyes come into their own.

The Place

The place where the floured hens
sat laying their breakfast eggs,
frying their bacon-coloured combs in the sun
is gone.

You know the place –
in the hawthorn hedge
by the wattle tree
by the railway line.

I do not remember these things
– they remember me,
not as child or woman but as their last excuse
to stay, not wholly to die.

Thistledown

Thistledown with its white spider-spokes
tests my windowpane –
i happened to pass
i'm looking in
this thing that is between us
is glass

i'm off now
can't stay
can't rest
away away
to break my white prick in
a dark lady's nest.

Season

There is nothing to be done
no stone of surprise to unturn
no leaf to start from the bare tree
no ripple to be born on the pond that is iced over
no bud to burst into flower
seedling weed to trespass
sun to visit and stay till a late hour
for the year at the locked iron gate has stopped dead
winter is here
summer is gone
there is nothing to be done.

Sunday Drive

A dialogue is not the best way
to contain and capture last Sunday
yet we were two that, unlike the seagulls, spoke words.
'Terns churr-churr. That is their sound,' you said. 'Sea swallows
birds with graceful flight diving and soaring like fish in air.
Their tails are like fishes' tails too.'

Under the trees the puppet-daffodils shook their heads
nodding agreement to a plan we knew nothing of. Their applause, approval,
guided by the wind, continued
after we were gone while the dark trees above rocked
slowly, solemn breves to the golden demi-semi-quaver tune.
I thought their heads would be shaken off and roll downhill
into the green valley. It was hard to believe that on a still day
the daffodils stood with heads bowed
in gold shock under their yolk of calm.

You said as you started the car and drove away
'There may be only a week left in which to see them.
They will be dead soon.'

Dead, over, gone. How we accept it, in flowers!
We come in season to stare and go away murmuring
'The show is better than ever this year.'

Around the bay the waves were dark, crested with white,
like creatures moving alive under a wide blue blanket
with nobody warning them, Keep still!
Small waves trying to climb too high to see over the heads of those in front,
dark periwinkle waves, blue-skirted above a funnel of snow
with the wind sucking the honey of sound through.

Wallflowers along the clay bank, taking a warm glowing hold
with suncolour and smell and (more practical)
with summer root, velvet cloaks wound
buttoned against the inquisitive wind.

And then at the bach around the bay
we stopped to rest and eat and talk
and imagine the city hills misted with dark virgin bush
before you and I and we and they and they came.
We knew how the land appeared then. We remembered
as we remember clearly the world before birth
when waterfalls touched our skin and we grew, thinking, first
we might be a tree or tadpole until the oppression of knowing
surged in us refusing to set us free
from what we had begun to be.
Now only parts of us, like our thoughts, glow, are glossed with sun and fall
brittle in shapes of dust
as leaves do, giddy leaves growing first on a green tree.

Sheltered from the sea-wind we lazed and looked.
You chuffed a lawnmower over the grass
then served lemonade and crushed orange, measuring fair levels
in bottle and cup as if it were childhood we had driven back to.
'My favourite toy,' you said, 'was a tea set
kept out of reach, not belonging to me, of blue enamel; I thought my
heart would burst in its beating when I was allowed to pour out
tea from the tiny blue teapot with the question-mark spout.
And what was your favourite toy?'

'Mine,' I said, 'was a kerosene tin. I dragged it along in the grey dust
on a piece of string. It was shining and silver and hollow and it sang in the sun
and everything that touched it made it sing exclaim groan tingle cling-clang

gasp a tin gasp and proclaim
its sound and shape and glossy being
as an empty new kerosene tin that sang and mirrored the world.'

'Everything is always changing,' you said.
'A tree does not want to be anything but a tree.
Hands are better than wings; hands can fly.
Everything changes. The dead clematis on that tree is a burden to it.
It's like an old man with a sack on his back leaning towards the sea.
Hear the waves?'

I quoted,
'Palpitation de la mer.' A pulse beat.

'I would fight,' you said suddenly, 'if I were a child and my toys were taken away.
Would you fight?'

'As a child,' I said, 'I had few toys, no favourites, I cared most
for beetles and spiders, small cold creatures that lay
under stones, without sun.'

'How lovely the periwinkle loops along the criss-cross wire fence!
And the primrose flowering in the middle of the path. It was out
when we came here last. It is not dead yet.
Honeysuckle grows here.
There are four shelves of books in the sitting room. Poetry, the Old Testament.
I should like to stay here in winter, in the wild weather.'

'Would it not be too cold?'

'I should like to stay here when storms come out of the sea, and frost-ferns work
their stiff embroidery on the windowpanes.'

'Do you keep a diary?'
'I used to. I burned it. Do you keep one?'
'I do. Details I want to remember. Colours. A chance remark. A shape.'
'My diary, years ago, was of love; of smiles given
near and far away as the sun; of passionate beings
out of reach but shining faithfully, like planets.'

'Everything changes. Nothing will stay. My mother died four years ago,
and though I still do not mourn for her, I remember her.
Memory recurs, cripples. There is no relief from its pain.'

'Our parents are our first world. Do you remember
the childhood imagining of their death, of how it would be
with mother and father dead? How cruel winds came in

to take up the space they left, how exposed you stood
as on a headland, and could not bear the grief flowing
down down through your body to draw you into the earth?'

'I had no imaging of it. My mind and heart would not let me see it.
I closed myself against it like a flower closing against the night.'

'I saw it. Skipping,
Two little girls in navy blue
these are the actions they must do:
salute to the King,
bow to the Queen –
I would stop suddenly because my mother and father were dead
and there was no one above me to bend over me, there was nothing above me
save the sky.
Underchild, underdog, so happily under, and no one now to intercept
the hawk, the bogie, the charging bull, the glass words of people,
their hooked faces and their wire smiles,
their stiff geometric frowns.'

'No, I never saw it. I would not let myself see it. When the thought came
I made myself small and hid under a nasturtium leaf
and looked up, full of wise cunning, at the thin green rafters.
Oh, all is changing. All is different. Yesterday, today. Hear the terns?
Their cry is always churr-churr-churr
the repetitive deadening sentence;
but our words are not numbered; in crowds they come and go;
how I wish the few chosen would stay near,
close about us like threaded beads,
restricted like the cry of the tern!

'The day dazzles but is cold. Let us go home now.
It was like this and this and now it is not.'

'When people are toys you cannot fight to regain them.
They are gone. Let us put our perplexity and pain
in the sack of dead clematis that the old man tree
swings
        towards
                the sea.'

A Poem

There is a poem like a young willow
in the first days of spring, a thread
of green sago on a bead-string,
but certain, predetermined
as the numbered chromosomes
that sway unshattered by
the furious undercurrent of heredity.

There is a poem vanishing like a kite-tail
high in the sky; concealing,
like darning wool,
the hole in Achilles' heel;
parcelling with string
the birthday present and the clothes left behind
salt-filled, in the crib after the summer holiday.

There is a poem, a shape
of beads, bells or chains
not yet worn, rung or imprisoning, but waiting
till the season of words comes round again
and the fruit is ripe and the cider golden
and the drunken poet starts to sing.

Question

Wayward as dust when the wind blows around corners
into blind eyes; petrifying as stone
that sinks the heart of thistledown.
Grave as gravity denied
supremacy in outer space,
tall metaphor, explain me,
describe my shape.

Instructions for Bombing With Napalm

naphthalene coconut oil
health
a neat lethal plan
a late net
an alp at panther heap
a pale ten-pin heel lent to plant help
to pelt
at nether halt
at nether halt
hell

concoct ointment
ultimate oil
unction
lotion

count coil
act lout to that tune in loin
toil out then
lick the lion's lap
cut the lint
pal

O Lung Flowering Like a Tree

O lung flowering like a tree
a shadowy bird bothers thee
a strange bird that will not fly away
or sing at break of day and evening.

I will take my knife
I will cut the branch of the tree
he clings to and will not let go
then the wide sky can look in
and light lay gloss
on the leaves of blood beating with life.

Oh yes, tomorrow I will take my knife
and the light and I will look in,
O plagued lung flowering like a tree,
said the surgeon.

Yet Another Poem About a Dying Child

Poets and parents say he cannot die
so young, so tied to trees and stars.
Their word across his mouth obscures
and cures his murmuring goodbye.
He babbles, *they say*, of spring flowers,

who for six months has lain
his flesh at a touch bruised violet,
his face pale, his hate clearer
than milky love that would smooth over
the pebbles of diseased bone.

Pain spangles him like the sun.
He cries and cannot say why.
His blood blossoms like a pear tree.
He does not want to eat or keep
its ugly windfall fruit.

He does not want to spend or share
the engraved penny of light
that birth put in his hand
telling him to hold it tight.
Will parents and poets not understand?

He must sleep, rocking the web of pain
till the kind furred spider will come
with the night-lamp eyes and soft tread
to wrap him warm and carry him home
to a dark place, and eat him.

At Evans Street

I came one day upon a cream-painted wooden house
with a white bargeboard, a red roof, two gates,
two kinds of japonica bushes, one gooseberry bush,
one apple tree lately in blossom; and thus I counted
my fortune in gates and flowers, even in the white
bargeboard and the fallen roofbeam crying religiously to the carpenter,
Raise me high! and in this part of the city that would be
high indeed for here my head is level with hills and sky.

It is not unusual to want somewhere to live but the impulse
bears thinking about seriously and it is wise
never to forget the permanent impermanence of the grave,
its clay floor, the molten centre of the earth, its untiled
roof, the rain and sunbeams arrowing through slit
windows and doors too narrow to escape through,
locked by the remote control of death-bed convulsions
in a warm room in a cream-painted wooden house with
a red roof, a white bargeboard, fallen roofbeam... no, it is not unusual
to nest at my time of year and life only it is wisest
to keep the spare room always for that unexpected guest, mortality,
whose tall stories, growing taller, tell
of the seagull dwelling on bare cliffs, of eagles high
where the bailiff mountain wind removes all furniture (had eagles known the need
for chairs by the fireside – what fire but the sun?) and strips the hangings
from the trees; and the men, also, camouflaged as trees, who climb the rock
face and of the skylark
from whose frenzied point of view harvest is hurricane
and when
except in the world of men
did hurricanes provide shelter and food?

In my house I eat bread and wish the guest would go.

The Clown

His face is streaked with prepared tears.
I, with others, applaud him, knowing it
is fashionable to approve when a clown cries
and to disapprove when a persistent sourface
does whether or not his tears are paint.

It is also fashionable, between wars,
to say that hate is love and love is hate,
to make out everything is more complex than we dreamed
and then to say we did not dream it,
we knew it all along and are wise.

Dear crying clown dear childlike old man
dear kind murderer dear innocent guilty
dear simplicity I hate you for making me pretend
there are several worlds to one truth when
I know, I know there are not. Dear people like you and me
whose breaths are bad, who sleep in and rumble
their bowels and control it until
they get home into the empty house or among the family,
dear family, dear lonely man a torn world of nobody,
is it for this waste that we have hoarded words over so many
million years since the first sigh, groan,
and look up at the stars. Oh oh the sky is too wide to sleep under!

Vacant Possession

All day on the phone. All day
desperate for vacant possession,
ringing to find if the furniture has gone
have I moved it yet; if not, why?

How can I explain
that my dead mother's best bedroom and fireside suite
have first claim, that their obstinate
will is to remain. Proud beasts they stand.

Nothing will shift them out
but the voice my mother used when she spoke to her
companionable furniture.

Now her voice is gone and the house is sold and I do not know
the command that persuades a well-loved fireside suite
meekly to rise up on its casters and go!

The Garden

Japonica petals like yellow crumbs
and red japonica with waxed petals;
hedgehogs snuffling, and in the road
outside a dead hedgehog and its blood
like fuchsia petals.

I chopped off the heads of the grass. I had
a clear memory of what was lost –
the glittering spectacle of morning,
of grass going to the opera at the wrong time
beyond reason yet in rime and rhyme.

Furious in the delicate vulnerable
garden what else could I do?
I had to make it mine,
to eat the yellow crumbs scattered among
the leaves as if I had been
a bird in winter, to kill the common
green grass that wilfully put on its crown
jewels in the morning.

Then my unease was gone,
I thought my battle for possession won.
I reckoned without the overworld sun
that burgling every strong-room
holds, keeps man, woman, house, garden,
to drop all one night
in the well
without a ripple.

Rain on the Roof

My nephew sleeping in a basement room
has put a sheet of iron outside his window
to recapture the sound of rain falling on the roof.

I do not say to him, The heart has its own comfort for grief.
A sheet of iron repairs roofs only. As yet unhurt by the demand
that change and difference never show, he is still able
to mend damages by creating the loved rain-sound
he thinks he knew in early childhood.

Nor do I say, In the travelling life of loss
iron is a burden, that one day he must find
within himself in total darkness and silence
the iron that will hold not only the lost sound of the rain
but the sun, the voices of the dead, and all else that has gone.

Crusts

Crusts upper and lower
brown and white
turn destruction
                into light
crack the sun
              that cracked the wheat
feed the people in famine street.

Comment

Smell of sweat in the armpits dismays more
than the distant smell of the dead in a jungle war.
Possible and important are the blind date and alley but not
the blind man and his plight.

Heaven is curls in place
guipure over fine embroidered lace, leather
simulated, not mind membrane, human
skin woven together on an unknown face.

A clanger dropped at afternoon tea
is more shocking than a plane-load of bombs on Hanoi.
The cancelling of a rugby match through rain
is more lamented than the cancelling of a thousand men.

So let us cheer for our strange worldly wisdom in knowing
how to pack into our life's thrilling journey
such little happinesses that keep us determinedly going
to hell and back!

A Visit to the Retired English Professor

There in the grovertangle where sun-coltering stilth
galed down, splurned, merged into riper than cleamhold
warmermaze when its skin streakles pomperwelling in summer,
we flindered, melled, wimwalling, hintered.
                                        Clone,
plene in his rale after so calid a time had milled its fee,
durant, he burndered, cleamed in the day's coltering zone.

Then we sat under the plum tree
on the wet grass-covered stone
while he talked of Hamlet.

The Family Doom

This gene is bred, cradled like my own son,
Heredity said when I demanded to know how
the family doom stays unchanging in its dugout
safe and snug while storms of sporting winds blow.

My time is too old, Heredity said,
to care for the half-million other traits
like happiness, that drift like thistledown in every sporting wind
while Doom, faithful homebody, stays.

Wet Morning

Though earthworms are so cunningly contrived
without an opposing north and south wind
to blow the bones of Yes apart from the flesh of No,
yet in speech they are dumbly overturning,
in morning flood they are always drowned.

This morning they are trapped under the apple tree
by rain as wet as washing-day is wet and dry.
An abject way for the resilient anchorage of trees,
the official précis of woman and man,
the mobile pillarbox of history, to die!

Once

Once the warm draught of people
flowing under the locked door that held me from them
changed my flame, played
influence on my shadow,
burned re-burned me where I made
my tablets of wax in the dark.

Then beyond the door all was still.
Thief blackbird stopped up the keyhole
where birdbeaks of light, comforting, had pecked crumbs through.
A winter I could never know
sealed the cracks with an evil they called snow.
It was so pure, falling
from nowhere, its flakes blinding.

Beyond the door all was still.
I leaned in my lonely ritual.

The Sun Speaks at Perihelion

On the twelve Christmas days
I thought my gift and your treasure
would be my shining closest to earth.
Why did spires gouge out my eyes?
Why did the television crucifix
mingle my blood
with dancing girls, the Truth Game,
and the criss-cross Quiz of Christ?

Atom

Now the blossom is sucked clean.
The bees policed in iron hives
control confuse threaten
the uncombed sweetness with power
to take lives by flash and fire.

It was in invisible flower
the nectar of worm and birth
an idea come up for air.
Iron bees, is it for new bread
or death the sweetness is spread?

Haworth Parsonage, Mt Maunganui
(for E.P.D.)

This house: five headstones – five or any number
of senses, of dead, of fingers of the left hand
or lost world not sharing the secret,
climb, strapped with sand, salt-fed, bloom
white, alive, upon a morning trellis of cloud,

make summer houses where the living
command the sun behind tall glass
to warm, not set fire to, their tombs' autumn covering;
for leaves burn, mirrors break, Gerda-grime here
as in treeless Yorkshire may enflame their eyes.

Though never the five dead coughing in fog
will feed this earth yet, white stone your parsonage,
the house with its guavas, a lemon tree, hedge plants
wrapped in paper shawls against the frost; dank weed, castaway log,
sea-drowned wapiti antler the flower's full provision.

I Knew a Man

I knew a man one long time
whose heart had no real home.
I recall that he walked with a spirit-level
ceaselessly uphill, downhill.

He carved for his heart a flat tomb
in the tussock, and for many years kept warm
as a new-killed rabbit, till
he died at length of the sun's chill.

My Home

O the cold unpeeled hood
of my mushroom home
where sheep lie at night
on the warm oven-shelf of hillside
facing away from the south and the south wind
that on March days will drive
a comfortless other flock
of thistledown,
turned out of house and home
given the white sack
with winter for last wage,
from summertime!

When the Sun Shines More Years Than Fear

When the sun shines more years than fear
when birds fly more miles than anger
when sky holds more bird
sails more cloud
shines more sun
than the palm of love carries hate,
even then shall I in this weary
seventy-year banquet say, Sunwaiter,
Birdwaiter, Skywaiter,
I have no hunger,
remove my plate.

Some Will Be for Burning

Some will be for burning, not all.
In the deep sky trees may lean, and men,
to take their hot gold coin, and some,
not all, will be for burning.

In autumn many trees have ashes for leaves;
the willow and the silver poplar
have paid the penalty of fire
no creek or soft rain will smother;
and there are men whose footfall on earth
is like the smoke and whisper of leaves.

But some will be staying cold and whole
like stone in growth of moss, the green ember
kindled by creek water and soft rain.

Thought

Parsons and racegoers
bleed to death pondering.
The sea till millennium's thirst
walks up and down the platform
impatient for the tide.

Tadpole

By frog I have escaped the indrawn teeth of black eel,
the long room of duck's mouth. Were I a man
should I not dance, leap, sing, prepare a five-year plan
or twenty-year or thirty till the sun burn through my soul?

But I, being soon frog only, how shall I explain
myself to myself, or tell of the dead year,
the escape from death in dark birth-circle of water,
the blackout into croaking light of my only plan?

Prejudice

Somebody has been in the bath too long,
somebody must soon pull out the plug,
drain away the dirty seas
scour the tidemarks from the coast
and with a secret ingredient (like truth)
dissolve the flotsam of old drowned bones
that were used as toys to distract, escape
from bathwater oceans of ideas that have got too dirty and too deep.

Her Thoughts

Her thoughts like poppies go to sleep in their clothes
with no west wind to iron out the creases in the morning.

The Sun

1

Now the sun
dark red
ladled across a bleak distance
shines warm
as evening cocoa
in an old man's home.

2

The sun
is a universal
shining
bank messenger
with a consuming inner life
and an Honours Degree in Perspective.

Dialogue

'People are strange?'

'Yes. They gave the rat of fear a brilliantine hairdress,
smoothed its bristle, preened its whiskers.
Clean and harmless as an ultra-bomb or refined plague
it followed like a poodle at the heels of their God.

'For exercise it walked upon the faith-lit Common
Ground of superstition; for breeding purposes it used
the free steepled stud opposite the Town Hall, the reserved
shelves of libraries, and cinemas showing expurgated films.

'How it earned the approval of their domestic hearts!
But – secret in the night, as the Rat of Fear, it gnawed
the stale furred slices of love, the half-tasted meal,
the torn letter of demand, refusal, transition,
all the overflowing garbage of their guilt.'

'People are strange?'

'Yes, after the indifference of bees and lions
to small print, fossils, promises and disaster funds.'

These Poets

These poets command the familiar working of
their merry-go-round of words and postures known.

Their pony or wild tiger syllables hop
terribly up and down in usual tune.

May quick Caesarian insight bring them word-cub
whimpering; toppling foal of poem one moment born.

Snow

A crime so frequent, so huge
of fraud and camouflage
would make it seem almost natural
the hurt world lying forever
                              locked in plaster
with some remembering the green
                                    underneath,
others never forgetting the
                        fracture.

Furniture

Idiots are not all a smile and a wide plain
with the sun concentric in their eyes;
but a straw room, food to sleep with,
a stairway to straddle, and all belonging
put back to their secret mouth.

They do not talk wisely like wise men,
though wise men,
seeing the uncluttered room of an idiot
may envy him his wisdom in not knowing three things –
how to compare,
how much furniture should have been there,
and where it has gone.

People Are Ill, Dying

People are ill, dying. The skin
like that of a mushroom
is peeled from the flesh. The body
is not poisonous after all.

It sprang up overnight
under the sky in a dew
where a warm sheep
snuggled asleep
and in its centre stalk
a worm lay.

Mysterious night origins
rain of centuries of hate
dung and dew
the worm in the pillar
the ceiling of flesh
the sun on the roof.

Is this proof
that man is an edible fungus,
a mere breakfast treat
to be fried by bomb's explosion,
eaten by nothingness of death?

Dunedin Walk

Today as I walk through the Botanical Gardens
I think of Nikita Khrushchev and the peasant sayings he might have found in
Dunedin.

'It is better to keep a rogue elephant as ornament in your front window
than a live pine tree with its roots aching in your heart.'

'With every sting a bee perishes. Death is more alkaline
than baking soda and its formula is always variable.'

'Ducks on a muddy pond may not be numbered accurately. The curse
of arithmetic is that it thrives in stillness,
its true focus is seen only in death.
Do not be deceived by the pool's irrelevance.
Men as well as ducks are amphibious creatures.'

'There was an old man, a Hillside Worker, who once glimpsed the Governor
General.
Is he entitled to a smile and handshake fifty years later?
Representatives are not people
except when they touch. Then there is proof
they have skin that renews itself every seven years
and freckles and burns in the sun.'

'It is not the agony of the poor dead or the dead poor
that they cannot butter their bread
only that they may not eat or talk or kiss.
It is the agony of the living
the dead should grieve like this
when winter is solely dependent on
the willingness of green leaves to die.'

'A sound shell where a brass band plays
only on fine days and holidays
is like a sheep farmer
who goes to the wool sales
to sneer at the fleeces of his own flock.'

Mother and Son

My mother said to my brother, 'Dearest child
that you may not choke and die
I will cut your meat into small pieces
I will remove the bones from the chicken and the fish
that you might eat without fear:
                                   that is my wish.'

'Mother, mother, a strange meal approaches, too huge
with too many bones.
                       It is pushed before me
on a plate as wide and round as the sky
on a table of grass and forest.
                             Our cupboard never held
a knife to slice it nor had you hands to tear
the flesh apart from so many bones growing thick as trees.
O mother, mother, I will choke and die!'

My mother said to my brother, 'Dearest child,
is your meal so strange and fearful?
                                   It is I.'

The Kea Speaks from the Dunedin Botanical Gardens

I have learned to walk upside down like a fly
while my neighbour three cages away cries, Woe O Woe.
I can sense, though not see, the sky.

I too, like you, have a ceiling of wire to my aspirations,
while the peach-faced lovebirds huddle together close to the earth
and the wekas move like small brown brooms through the rushes.

If you were to write a poem about me you would say, Pity
the kea's imprisonment. But it would be yourself you pitied
in your own prison, for though you can both sense and see the sky
you have not yet learned to walk upside down like a fly.

Dunedin Story

I brought a leper into my house.
I gave him the spare room with the panel-end bed, the flock mattress, the spare
                                                   blankets and sheets
and the duchesse with the oval mirror
that, swinging back and forth, reflects a person from head to foot.

'I have travelled a long way,' my leper said.
'I had to wait many years before they gave me a permit to come here.
I had to be investigated, examined,
sponsored,
and then at last
I was accepted.
I shall get treatment here from the hospital on Cumberland Street.
I shall sleep in your spare room, have meals with you,
walk down through the Botanical Gardens under the Ponderosa pine trees
across the bridge
past the Otago Savings Bank Centennial Kiosk
past the pensioners' houses in Duke Street.
And then one day when I am cured I will go to the Labour Exchange and find
                                                   a job.
How happy I am to be accepted into your country!'

The neighbour clipping his hedge looked over at me.
'I hear you've a leper staying with you,' he said. 'Isn't it dangerous?'
I answered with the best argument.
'Oh they wouldn't have admitted my leper if they thought that,' I said.
'You know they're very careful about that sort of thing.'
'I suppose you must be right,' my neighbour said. 'All the same
I'd watch out if I were you.'

The woman tending the deep-freeze in the grocer's lifted the
steak and egg sausage carefully out of its
bed beside the chicken and onion sausage.
'I hear you've a visitor,' she said. 'Is he staying long?'
'Oh he's making his home here.'
'He's from overseas?'
'Yes. My leper. He's come to be cured.'
The woman frowned. 'Yes, I've heard that,' she said.
And after I began to walk from the shop I noticed she rubbed her hands
on a small towel hanging on a rail behind the door.

The front of my house reeked of disinfectant.
Men from the Council
had arrived and were cleaning the footpath.

182

'The city's taking no chances,' the foreman said.

Months passed. Spring came, and summer, and autumn, and winter
when the rain stayed clogged in the long grass and the dead
leaves flapped against the twigs
and fog, mingled with smoke, settled like snow in the valleys.
My leper was stricken with a strange disease
that no one could diagnose.
It was, they said, a disease worse than leprosy, worse than any other,
hardest to be cured of,
a fatal disease where the sufferer may yet last a lifetime in agony and humiliation.

They said he had caught the disease from the neighbours cutting the hedges,
from the woman serving in the deep-freeze counter in the grocer's,
from the Council men spraying disinfectant outside my front door,
and – worst blow of all – they said he had caught it from me,
from my use of the possessive pronoun.
'Did you not talk of him,' they reminded me, 'as *your* leper?
My leper, you said. *My* leper this and that.
The disease of being at once outlawed and owned is worse than leprosy.
It is, simply, terribly,
the indestructible virus
the gift of the living who are blind
to the living who are believed dead.'

Dream

Tiny people in a tiny tilled field
(which God can hear the grass grow?)
my teeth in black cases were black
like coffins; I had eaten
dates that stuck to my teeth; I had
eaten time and hastened my own decay.
Which God can hear the grass grow
and the wool on a sheep's back?

Cat Spring

At this time of year strangers lurk in my garden.
Their cry gobbles the snow-encircled full moon,
their alley-hunger makes a sexual slum
of a city that is rumoured to be clean. I
                                    never trust
                                              rumour.

Beware, Dunedin!
                  The cats are out of the bag at last.
                                              The chambers
of night commerce are full
                        to overflowing.
It is spring.
            The gardens hold immeasurable loot
                                        of gold
crocuses, silk-
            veined daffodils
                        stained lust of
                                  tomcats'
                                        milk.

Born in a Gentle Country

Born in a gentle country
mothered by peace and mercy
I've never learned to stay in the forbidding House of Judgement
where guests are warned to speak one sentence only,
'Humanity is no excuse for Humanity.'

I've discovered it's not mercy
nor peace nor being born in a gentle country
that deters me: the rent is too high
decision on decision paid out to a total
terrifying life-long responsibility.

Besides, who is to know whether the true owner, Love,
who first toiled and planted the walled garden, may
wander now,
himself an insane prisoner in the House of Judgement?

Beginnings

Up the crocuses,
and they are struck down;
up the crocuses again
old-gold, and they dare not open.

I'll not see them this year,
their first year in a new bed,
tangled in the cold sheets of the earth
enforced guests of the sleeping sun

that refuses to wake into light and prepare breakfast.
O struck down
broken at the stem
their magnificent heads wound in a golden scarf.

Up the crocuses
to try a third time
one morning to feed
their innocent faces with light?

Early Spring

Nothing doing
except at the foot of the stem
closest to earth
a rub of green leaf

almost in bloom;
a winter-lost bud
found, clothed again by the storm
of memory's green dust.

Poets

Poets are not afraid to drown.
The dry people of the dry world walk on
wanting to dive in yet not having learned
to swim or administer mouth-to-mouth breathing.
The poet is a poor fish, they say. Leave him.

O Tom Dick and Harry
Mabel Mildred and Cora
what is that tide flowing out of the room and into the street?
Somebody's best-kept words have got out.
We are in danger of wet feet!

O Tom Dick and Harry
Mabel Mildred and Cora
from foot to ankle to thigh
(Oh! hot on the scent of me, a rude noun!)
higher and higher the tide is flowing

and we are not fish rich nor poor
and we can neither swim nor drown.

Wyndham

The big stick
has given up stirring
the Wyndham pool.

Stones do not move here;
people sleep while
the cows make milk
the sheep make wool

and in the empty
railway houses
no Dad sits each morning
on the satin-smooth
dunny seat.

Duties

To buy a shank of mutton
for an old widow-woman
who lies in bed sick
with an aching back.

To cook the shank of mutton
with a carrot and an onion
a turnip and potato
while the fire burns low.

To serve a bowl of soup
to do the washing-up
to smooth the ruffled bed
and the pillow at her head.

To fill the coal scuttle
put out the milk bottle
hook that latch tight
of the creaking gate.

Then look in on Monday
Tuesday Thursday and on Sunday
on Wednesday and on Friday
to keep her house tidy

then to gaze at her slyly
and not wonder why
with her life run dry
she fails to die.

Flo

Flo's dead.
Go down, God.
Magnificent with curses
with judgment
the Moving Finger points
and having pointed
not all your delicate death announcements in the newspaper
your hiding of the fact
that she died you know where
in a back ward mad
can alter her white-haired splendour as I knew her –
spokeswoman for God (who else ever dared?)
commanding with her mountain frown
the cruellest world ever made to Go Down, Go Down
the dark Well
of Hell
and Drown.

This Is the Forest

'This is the forest primeval, the murmuring pines and the hemlock.'

These are part of my life's takings
from the till of word-mystery.
Cream salt-seeds of hemlock syllables
drop in my hair and lap
and in my body's and mind's eye.

Congregations lean their heads to pray
for brown cloth books of needle-words
to mend the earth, for God-sway haloed
with blue sky. Let me out:
the darkness is a cry of birds.

Merchant of Mammon and Prayer I sold
the longlasting aniseed sun
and bought a new disconsolate world
of wordless murmuring
wailing where nothing new is known

where drawn beneath the rust-stained blanket
the perfect sentence of sleep lies
wrapped in dark word-earth of forests.
Ripe cones bursting feed bright
speech-rockets to the silent fires.

The Chrysalids

As a child not more sensitive than others
I used to pick the grey-walled chrysalids
for fishing bait, and afterwards feast well
on the rainbow and brown trout my father caught.
Now, exiled from the crawling flying creatures
that once mistook my hair for red shrubbery,
barley grass, a mossy forest, I feel compassion
for the world I robbed. I remember those windowless
grey houses of sober unusual design;
hanging dungeons dependent on the frail
life-security of attachment to leaves;
houses with walls grey-folded, pleated
like robes of monks; frayed hairshirts,
old sackcloth sealed at top and tail; dull
colonies and clusters that never showed light;
deep shelters with the occupants asleep,
unable to receive or comprehend
the wildfire rumour spreading from red leaf
to red leaf that the world was nearing its end,
that a new world, in seclusion, was being made complete.

I did not know. I would never have believed
that every house I stole contained a jewel.
I gathered them as if they had been over-ripe fruit,
I thought their mud-coloured walls withered
and ugly and useful only for fishing bait.
And now I feel compassion. Is it too late
to soften to a new shape and dimension the hard truth
that parallel worlds must never meet?

The Pocket Mirror

So many thousand times a minute
the light from the street lamps goes out.

I have devised a method by which this may be shown
to those to whom the facts of light are unknown.

Taking this pocket mirror, capture the reflection
of the row of lamps. Steady the mirror. So.

See those black stripes alternating with yellow?
They are bars of actual darkness not perceived by the naked eye.

To undeceive the sight a detached instrument like a mirror is necessary.
The human senses never speak the truth if they can get away with an easy lie.

Tigers on the prowl? Tar spread with butter?

Master Dark
in his sergeant's coat?

A black cat on a bed of cheese?
Goldfinch feathers? Clay and cypresses? A sandwich of Heaven and Hell?
Caterpillars looping the length of street
feeding on darkness to become morning butterflies?

What can I say but that you are burdened with lies.
You babble of sunpollen, honey-plight
of black tulips; you repeat that you *know*
when you are clearly ignorant of the facts of light
and intend to remain so.

Wait! Give me back my pocket mirror. Were it to break
I should have no clear sight, and seven years' bad luck!

At Night

At night across my window I see
the shadow of a stair and a tossing tree.
I know they are really there, outside,
but I am afraid.

The moon shining down
splinters the roofs of the town;
the street-lights in glory
that is awkward and without reward
and does not make plants and people grow,
stand alone revealing the emptiness,
varnishing the grey streets with unrequited light
that is a desert festival,
a banquet that no one wants to eat.

Lying half-asleep I am spring cleaning
the lived-in quarters of my dreaming.
I throw away the horror and fear
(I think) beyond the window, but they stay,
they stay there in the shadow on the blind
of the nameless tossing tree and the dark stair.

O the harm of harmlessness,
the leaking guilt that makes a morass
of innocence until at last
sleep, like swamp lilies, blossoms there!

Country Dead

Except in times of epidemic and war
the sight of human remains is rare.
White-skulled cattle with splintered horns,
hips of sheep, huge horse-flanks like shovels,
chicken wishbones
– these provide the image of human friend, family and stranger who die
– I mean, in our country.

In childhood they said, Take Uncle Henry's dead hand.
I never held it as I held closely
the rabbit's paw until the fur had rubbed off,
though Uncle Henry also lay caught in a shining oblong trap
and was thrust out of sight in the cold earth
and the world's weather never had a chance
to set Uncle Henry or anyone I knew, polished and clean
in tussock, matagouri, snowgrass,
as properly finished dead people of bone.
It was only surmise that made their image, in the dark,
resemble the lost animals I had known
who surely lounged upstairs sunbathing their grey skulls and growing
grass hair in a permanent golden wave and wearing
white mushroom sun hats each morning new.

O the brazen extravagance of the country dead!
Aunties May, Lily, Marigold and Uncle Henry.
Aunties May, Lily, Marigold, and Uncle Henry!

Beach

Here is an empty bulb of transparent jelly
whose light swam within; we regret
our houses are not such even with ceiling to floor
glass windows nor are we our own illumination,
yet we stay, we do not abandon house
to return to the sea that abandoned us
as flick-knife brain unfolding to cut through cell walls
and form some attachment to growing.
                              Sea grapes
cluster white on the white sand. Wave on wave tills the old vineyard; kelp
carcasses, amber and green armour still worn shifting
the dead thing from upper to lower wave in expectation of
battle of tide grenades foam-bursting blossoming
to crush what tries to grow or having died to move even after death,
to join the commotion of going that waves are, eternally.
Eternally?
            Caution putting a sheltering hand over this word
to stop it like a candle flame from going out
(though who uses candles now?) commands, Don't. Let the word be, in its
                                        corner of the world
burning for ever, being what it is, without energy for sentences.

                          Some seaweed
cast out of the sea though not outcast
is like lace woven into leaf patterns; some is like a forest
of dead bulls with horns still waving.
We walk on the sand. We do not make three-toed footprints.
How proud we are, then, of our five toes!
Dogs run, bark at the sea, leave their forked prints; gulls fold,
unfold, their paper wings poised
beyond the green glazed window.

School is not out. Four-square country school, the iron-skirted
bell swinging aloft, the dental clinic smell,
the playground caved and pitted as if asphalt in geological guise
tries against time to record time
beside the venerable sea rocks skipped on, played on
by generations of waves dancing, stamping impatient sun-filled idleness.

A woman hastens with late afternoon shopping, otherwise
the street beside the sea is deserted. The curtains are drawn
in the white holiday houses.
In the gardens young plants battered beyond their years lean
on manuka sticks and taste their tears returned by the wind and spray.
                          The tide is almost in.
No rockpools. No shells. Only the thunderous display
of waves deceptively smooth suddenly on nearing the shore
giving up the tremendous ghost of their blossom
over and over and over, dragging a groan heavy, entangled as seaweed
from the throat of the watcher.
                          The groan
is the only language that without thought
will encompass the meaning.

Thinking will, in time, unravel the ancient knot of despair.
                          Words
will drop like pearls from the sheltering loops.
It is writers rather than boyscouts who must investigate the culture of knots, learn
to pitch words by the sea, to make
fire with less than two vowels rubbed together
and name it other than this groan of despair.

Jungle Fruit

A snake is hissing in the undergrowth
but I am safe: I have eaten the jungle fruit.
Snakes are patterned like linoleum
but without flowers, and polished
by the absent sun into diamonds and circles
that startle with danger; but I am safe
I have eaten the jungle fruit.

The first time it was bitter and I spat it out.
The second time the taste of it made tears come to my eyes.
The third time I tried to swallow it whole and then
it stuck in my throat
and I was dumb for seven years and a day and night.

I am speaking now in the sunlight and firelight
in the green world while the snake's head
golden and flat as a penny
lies unspent among the stones.

Dying

Dying, the accountant who skated
on thin ice was rated
an Obituary in the morning paper
(the *Otago Daily Times*)
that made no mention of crimes
called him neither embezzler nor raper
but told of his various memberships sailing
to charitable waters
and how he left a young widow wailing
and one son and two daughters.

In a career of managing pounds and pence
he should have accumulated enough sense
(forty is a mature age)
to heed the warning advice:
Beware. No skating. Dangerously thin ice.

Or was his death simply a final marriage
of principle and practice?

The Spell

Into one medium-sized sliced-pineapple tin
left overnight to gather North East Valley household
smoke, and fog surrounding the green farm on the valley slope
where each morning sheep bleat and dogs bark,
put one thread of crocus budded two days, one frost petal from a south-facing
windowpane, one flame from a garden bonfire
one beam from a peak-hour television programme,
enough light to flood, darkness to fill
the four leaks in the kitchen roof that will never be mended.

Then taking as much as a skyful of Swampy Clouds,
a haul that everyone will say is impossible,
geranium-red clouds, tussock-brown, silver and pearl, seagull colour,
bomb-shape, blossom-shape, stir
and over the brew keep watch all night with rain
until the spell erupting into vivid morning
miraculously overflows the pink and white terraces of sky,
and light, on inspection, descends,
gentle with early daffodils but flashing crude
mirrors to date more precisely the wrinkled
local specimens of human skin.

The time drops into history and the history books.
Questions are asked – What was the picture of life before the Spell?
Within dying memory was it all so cruel?
No one wants to remember.
The green and gold lava of spring has set,
                                    completing
                                            the burial.

A Golden Cat

As I walked to my office one day and stopped
by the flax bushes near the curve of the road
to look at the view of the city and North East Valley
and the amber poplars with the light shining through them,
and all the autumn trees turning where turn still means decay,
the souring of the once freshly foaming season,

a golden cat came out of the bushes, wove
around my feet, said, Own Me, Own Me, I am golden.
Scorched flax, leaves, berries on fire, none
come so gracefully to you; it is I
who am the weaving golden season.

I hurried on thinking perhaps I dreamed it.

Mother and Daughter

Gay strawberry tassels hang from the arbutus.
Irresistibly persuaded, raindrops separate
from clinging leaves. Water easily will let go
its trembling hold when earth-force reaches up to tug it free.

Half-green, half-yellow, the sycamores are shabby with waiting.
Their windmill seeds, knowing
the routine, travel blindfold past withered
stalks that languidly admit, It can happen here.

Custom lies heavier than death upon the scene.
The watching eye must look away to discover
Proserpine ugly, unpredictably human,
abhorring white lilies, roses, saffron flowers,

while her mother, blonde Ceres, does not care so late
to tramp cornfield and street to discover where
in what underground hovel with whom
her wayward daughter sleeps six months of the year.

Yet concern and love are told still in the moss-burning strawberries
and the young raindrops, without will, sliding into the earth
and the wind awake all night, helping in the search for what is lost
and the glistening white face of the frost against the morning window.

Lament for the Lakes

The colback talkus
the lacklegion worcle
the dindle pyrrage
all in fusive query have tanquished
the plion's domacious thrave.

Barevolved, craffhanded, turbuked
under driftices of berge
damperly they have sultured
mormed without crumbience or zone
each tressled pave.

How often the clamber has grined
murplained in full bondary and plexment
against roamage, thorm strild
vout sordure disencloming the dupely lakened seethe!

Circumless dranion has cunneived
has tranced it without requining
where only the pribed sparrion
crope turbly crysically
the rigilant endeethe

and angletamed with armile
the dislatched wolmew clangs
heedily this downage ominime
in foil and bondary, murplains from grope
to grope its alpave

where at furmess, dragly com, wim
with magerman strifle
still the colback talkus the lacklegion worcle
the dindle pyrrage
brackly tanquish the plion's thrave.

The Cabbages

The leaves that sheltered the cabbage heart became
coarse, thick veined with the labour of growing.
They lay flat, covered with dust, invisibly seamed
to the tough low-squatting stem that, knuckled and notched,
still lived to remind the blind root that after
the tender heart has been cut out cabbages still grow.

Fate is a consuming snowfall of white butterflies, a cow's
hoof crushing, torn leaves thrust through the wire netting into the fowl run
to be pecked at, eaten.
                Winter.
                      All the cabbages have gone
save a few battered leaves. Each plant that gave without protest
its newly formed heart, its core of being, its growing reason,
receives the blessing of emptiness and age:
frost on a grey head;
a long thirst satisfied
by glinting dewfall
returned again and again
to the sun, as treasure.

The Suicides

It is hard for us to enter
the kind of despair they must have known
and because it is hard we must get in by breaking
the lock if necessary for we have not the key,
though for them there was no lock and the surrounding walls
were supple, receiving as waves, and they drowned
though not lovingly; it is we only
who must enter in this way.

Temptations will beset us, once we are in.
We may want to catalogue what they have stolen.
We may feel suspicion; we may even criticise the décor
of their suicidal despair, may perhaps feel
it was incongruously comfortable.

Knowing the temptations then
let us go in
deep to their despair and their skin and know
they died because words they had spoken
returned always homeless to them.

Poem of Sight

Fore –
juts brow, shelf
intruding-most self,
skin closes
petals over roses,
cast arm, court and father
go and gather
hand-gift, lock and head,
name shore and noon-mast peak.

Eye –
blinkful
lashful tooth-wink
witness-glass brow-bath
sore shot and service.

In –
born and breathe,
deed-firm
flame land and roadside;
patient, tend and set urn
complete.

The Flowering Cherry

These cherries are not wine-filled bowls for thirsty birds
nor ornaments of the house where sky's the ceiling.
These are the pawnbroker tree's discreet sign,
the wine, tear and blood drops of bondage,
the tree's relentless advantage
taken of the poverty that came when, warmed
with familiar memory of what had been
and had been and would be but is never known
entirely or believed until it is born,
we saw the cherry tree in flower and at once spent
a life's rich astonishment.

'Why should I be bound to thee?'
Blake asked of the myrtle tree. Why?
He killed to escape. Blood flowed beneath the tree:
a father's blood, an old man's, who must have known
how to bargain with all possession
that makes a tree, a house, a sky into a prison
and each man see the marks of chains upon his skin.

The cherry tree flowers earlier than most,
falls as snow while snow is still falling,
sweeps into us and through us and we taste
the flower as fruit, we eat the first
full-blown light unfolded out of winter darkness.
Then, as if the bloom were gone, the tree will hide
in wine-coloured shade and pawn signs to pursue its trade.

And we are prisoners then, borrowing wonder
to redeem the pledge; or too poor, too ill,
too far away to make the necessary journey,
we plead in writing for the tree's mercy. Why
should a lifetime of marvelling be spent
on this first view of spring light, this burst of cherry snow?
Why should the tree house our treasure in blood?

When next you pass the flowering cherry now, in September,
look closely at the cool dark wine house
where the blackbirds sing for their supper
where the human senses sing for their survival.

Last Will and Testament

When collade wolders fail
when cabled I lie mead
then let this will be read,
my realty understood:

To Grapneline who loitered me
I leave my dimmer whurl.
To Grange, Able and Dully
my slate solstice pearl.

To Furner Done, my distant claim,
I leave my sendal humoursome
seniority of burying
with its churnel osmend harrowing.

To Larceny who fetted wing
wole and durstimion, a cilice thing
I leave – my new larch
to quinquilt his bones in March.

So much I have, so much I leave
when collade wolders fail.
Thus let my will be read,
my realty understood.

The Fahrenheit Man

The fahrenheit man
on the centigrade sea
with wittage and wantage
and wastage and me

filling the billen
with ices and tea
for Cynewulf's baggard
boggard, higgard
wittage wantage
wastage and me

the fahrenheit man
is so cruel to me
I paddle alone
on the centigrade sea
for wittage wantage
Cynewulf's baggard
boggard, higgard
have gone from me
to tropical summer
to simmer and shimmer
to quimmer and quammer

wittage wantage
wastage, Cynewulf's baggard
boggard higgard
the fahrenheit man
is so cruel to me
alone on the centigrade sea.

Had Man No Memory

Had man no memory:
a city without walls
no toll to pay
no promise to keep.
Sleeping, dreaming a safety
waking an honesty;
day devoid of dimness
night of trickery.

In home and street
the warm bread the cold stone,
the burning the chill simplicity
of love and hate made one
without boundary

had man no memory.

Photocopier in the English Department

A sound of pumping pumping
the pressure put on
increased
to draw up preserve wine
out of the clay lip
the stone eye
pupilled with fire.

Pupil of fire
photocopier
reproducing fire
at love-cost, blood pressure,
wet print the point
of word-burst.

The Dreams

My brother kept bantams coloured like straw-like copper beech leaves;
my sister kept a pet rabbit with a sensitive collapsible nose.
I kept nothing. Nothing stayed with me
not even snow when I put salt on its glossy white tail
sweeping against the windowpane
with soft floating promises
of obedient captivity,

not even the snail
when I helped it travel a million miles
with one movement of my hand
over dense grass and waste earth
where the robber thistles and highwaymen spiders were lurking,

not even the rescued foreign stamp
when I gave it a family home
a classified accepted understood valued life
on a clean page safe inside a catalogue,
or the dry pressed ragwort
united with its woolly bear caterpillar in a matchbox.
Nothing stayed.
Dust did not stay, nor shadows. Light,
quietly dissolving the iron bars
sun-melted the key,
splintered the wooden food bowls,
set warm with warning
of inevitable prison.

Then one day my brother's bantams with their heads chopped off
ran in a panic up and down the fowl house;
my sister's pet rabbit escaped and did not know
fear of the hawk and ferret.
The bantams, the rabbit died.
Snow remained free, and snails, caterpillars, stamps, dust,
light entering the sky on its own terms.

I was a child then. I turn the memory
while tonight it snows, but I no longer care
for soft promises, and salt is for rubbing into old wounds,
and it is time while snow still falls, to feed the dreams
that run in panic up and down my sleep
that escape at last and unwittingly make friends with the hawk.

Complaint

The motormower a giant wasp on the lawn
reminds me that my nerves are torn.

The TV shots through the wall
do but speak of a Western Hell.

The children's quarrels and cries
tell me where my hate lies.

The traffic changing gear,
the singer without voice or ear,

the loudspeaker from the factory next door,
remind me that I've been here before

in a time quiet enough to hear a thought
parting the tangled stalks of words, creep
soft-footed from the dark into the sure trap
of light, serene light, smooth light;

the splinters piercing the once-quiet spot
remind me that thought without quiet has no shape,
that there's no escape,
that I wish either noise or I were not, were not.

I Do Not Deny the Sun

I do not deny the sun
that denies me.
I leave the door open,
wheat on the table,
apples in the pantry.

I was warned from the first hour
that the sun did not care,
tearing seasons with his tongue
while maudlin snow ran down his cheeks;
that he snored in a deep white bed
and waking did not as we do
– tell his dreams and embrace callers.

Christmas and Death

Christmas and Death are hungry times
when only the foolish and the dying
with circumscribed vision of Here
learn complete praise, saying
Bravo Bravo to the Invisible.

Who knows to what in the small yard
sunless, the turkey gives violent praise?
Or the sick man spread
on a white plate in his diminishing world?

Three Black Mice

Three black mice with no name,
the equivalent of healthy men in their prime,
sat in a space rocket waiting to be fired.
(Had they been men they might have expired.)

Bred for the occasion – a happy breed,
plugged and wired and batteried,
they didn't run after the scientist's wife,
she didn't cut off their tails with the electric carving knife.

No, they died in the sky. See how they fly,
three black mice they fly so high
near the giant paw that cuffs the light
across ninety million miles of night.

The Footballer in the Small Room

Now he roars through an unlit stadium of silence.
A curve of pain in his head
corresponds to this teamless loneliest game
where his blood has less worth than orange juice,
and the spectator walls do not know his name.

Graduate

She lives in letters. She knows
the quote, the plot that suits,
the words that fit the moment
as fox gloves fit the fleeing fox
with golden brush and speckled poison
described by him and him and her. Squalid borrower
who dreams another's life, who lives
not under the sun but flat between
another's pages as the useful bookmark, the fringed self-centre.

Still she waits for the surprising pool
where nothing grows, no fish have swum before,
no reed or weed has stirred a hopeless dream
for already
        – 'the sedge is withered from the lake and no birds sing.'

Rain

The rain runs down the windowpane.
Like.

There's the Great Cliché crying again!

The Poet

Though the wheat is so beautifully puffed
the rice is ballooned and stuffed
and the world seems so much bigger
from a few to a marvellous crowd
of supers, the pushing and proud
with more push and pride and the prig growing prigger,
the poet still breathes with one lung
climbs a ladder of only one rung
shoots at stars with his hand off the trigger.

Matthew

It is Matthew dressed in sea wave, scarcely walking
for weeds about his ankles, his life willingly
set in the stocks of ocean, pelted with light,
with ripe leaves from inland trees,
grievance of sharp deserted shells.
Open the door to him and the Dog Night.

He will stand there pleading the innocence of salt and cockle tooth
though his life has savoured many tears from the biting tide.
Over his thin unwashed body, congealed sunlight,
the black and white defiances of grave and shell
minstrel his passionate reason to be: it is, interpret
all shapes of wave, shell, and gull in flight.

Clairvoyant for what lives and is not human
the black Dog Night at his heels he walks night and day
by this dead sea where, Arabs of summer, children
holidaymaking bring new ancient scrolls to light.

O bandit gull, nomad wave,
from babbling cave of dungeon to articulate man,
man weeping,
man walking upright!

Telephonist

Her sense of humour has no gold stop
or sweetly flowing channel.
Her heavy feet plough tweed
through a silk and lace paddock of earth
upturning pink daisies and hoppity mice
with no by your leave or remedial poem.

She can laugh with any farmer,
her arms akimbo, her mouth braying
the yokel burden of a woman
who slaps daylight on the back
who walks in her lace country
with every flea-bitten shaggy dog.

Yet for eight hours each day
in the swivelling city of concrete
the talking wire commands her loud mouth.
She becomes the vital link, the braying ass
bearing news of life and death
to the hungry starstruck city.

Gods

Who said Gods have no need to dream?
They dream darkest and most
their night eyes inflaming a realm
their waking weeps as lost.

Chafing through torture of control,
burning mastery, they serve;
sleeping in soul made mortal
embrace their human love.

The lonelier their peaks of cloud
the closer their dreams come
to warm plain and peopled hillside
– Gods most have need to dream.

The Dead

I have nothing to say to the dead
unless they approach me first.
It is their right to come to me
with a soft step, singing
or moaning as they please.

The dead cry all night under the trees.
I never tire of listening to them.
Sometimes I want to invite them in
to warm their hands by the fire
but nobody wants the dead inside,
especially not the living. Lock the door,
keep them out, they say,
or the next thing you know
they will overcome you with death,
they will feed from you, rob you,
tap your blood and your preserved memory.
The dead have no memory. A torn scarf
flows in and out of their head, controlled
by the wind of forgetfulness, not by the dead,

and where the end or the beginning may be
the dead do not know
who have no memory, no memory.

As I Walked Along the Street

As I walked along the street I heard
a transistor singing like a bird,
an advertisement from 4ZB
singing in the cherry tree.

I said, So high, so far away
you sing in the push-button sky.
Have you a message of faith and hope?
It said – Use Lily-Clean Soap.

And I was angry then and tried
to forget the transistor bird
but its voice came loud in the world so green
– With Hexachlorophine.

Then I smote the bird and I smote the tree
and the push-button sky fell down on me,
and dying I lay alone without hope
or faith or Lily-Clean Soap.

A Light Verse

Now here's an introduction to
the bear who lives inside the Zoo.
He lived in houses many years,
he was a man with hopes and fears,
he breakfasted on bread and honey,
he worked all week to earn small money,
he was a teacher quite contrary
in a state school secondary
who found one day he'd nothing left
of all material things bereft
including his most faithful wife
who suited him as fork to knife
or knife to fork it doesn't matter
upon the matrimonial platter
which is which, except that she
could cut him more convincingly
with words and ways – that poor young teacher
hacked and hagged in every feature!

He thought it best (as many do)
to go to live inside the Zoo.

Snowdrop

Snowdrop where the slugs chewed
your body in half,
the time has spread oil
your wounds to heal.

You and I will never know
this year's flower. It is
like a lost vision that will swell
to fill all seasons.

I hear the heavy white bell
begin to toll.
I see the sad procession move
towards the white cathedral.
The sun shining on the green spires
is so beautiful.

Another Country

Something the undertakers
do not choose to undertake
is to grow the tree
that provides the wood
for the coffin of man woman and child.

Small white coffins
thin as planks
like chocolate boxes go
down the slopes past the Stations of the Cross.

The sea out there is warm, filled with refuse.
In early morning the fishing boats cough their morning coughs.
The passage of provender is cleared:
God will provide.

Fish, fish,
what is your wish? Silver-shining
and no one can tell if you are dead or not.
You die,
your nerves stay dancing all night
to the lost tune of life.

Church bells toll. It was a child dead,
a marriage, a feast day.
Tomorrow the band will play,
the children twirl their skipping ropes under the eucalyptus trees;
the white dust will rise to cover their faces.

Janus

A God-like sentry, he focused the past and future,
he smiled double, spied quadruple,
pensioned childhood butterflies,
grew daisies on an old woman's grave.

His gaze divided, forever turning,
he never left or entered the room.
He spied for us. With his charity and rare deformity
he played the private eye observing time

while we enjoyed the feast. Our tomorrow's table laden
with cherries and wine (our charm of blood against hunger)
we cried gratefully in one breath, 'Bring the sentry wine,
bring the sentry wine. He spied for us!'

Yes, he spied for us. We killed him. He deserved his death
who uncovered our past and future crime.

A Painting by Colin McCahon

During Easter weekend in Dunedin
after the hammer has hammered
and the nails are driven in
my neighbour stands back satisfied
he has made a secure house.

I think there is a wind blowing
through walls, bringing rain
to sealed houses and weatherproof people
and aches into the long propelling bones
the bones that get my neighbour and me and you somewhere;
that grip, run, embrace, reach to take.

Two letters X and P I saw set down
in order, clean and white as bones
upon a neglected earth-page covered with fungus
like grey moss but the propelling letters shone through
also a thumbnail-nicked corner of the sky
while human heads leaned dark against the mountain.

X-pel, X-plode, X-press,
X-pire, punge and pyre and plain (will you?)
ornate in their loneliness
bearing their shape with pride locked together
Pity and Cross that is kiss, wrong, the lost unknown
the mark that tells the plague-flower is within and, blossoming,
will look out the window of
the hammered house made secure,
offering honey.

Some Thoughts on Bereavement

Loss that in its time caused much mourning
disbelief, bewilderment, crying:

the loss first of the first warm home with
breathing walls, confrontation of air

full of storm and travelling dust, and
no special place again anywhere

not even in death though urn and stone
carry persuasion of tenancy.

The first cry is Everything has changed.
The first glance is backward, the first thought

is compare. The bubble of time need not
enclose me. I will break it and go

where I used to be, in familiar
places. And the first shock is loss of

everything as if by fire or bomb
and never again will the loss be so deep.

We hold separate fragile lives.
The shuddering seismic years topple,

home, dreams, people, ideas, all.
My history? I remember loss

of my grandmother, just that she went
away and did not come back for tea.

Of my grandfather who was taken
out of the red front gate with the hand-hole

in it where the latch was and I peeped
through and the hearse with shining black like

the polished marble clock in the dining
room. Of Aunty Maggie who choked on

every cherry stone; it was her throat.
There was no treatment for it. She died.

These are deaths and causes. Bereavement
is after, when people do not come

home for tea and beds are not slept in
and clothes not worn again gather dust.

Bereavement is waiting, waiting for
a known death to be undone, a time

eating itself to excrete the past.
Bereavement is the handling of shreds

that once made a whole garment.
It is seeing in the street a face,

hearing a voice that no one alive
will claim again or show interest in.

Those who are bereaved feel the sense of
waste. For a time they go outside time

and sit crouched in one place with their mouth,
their eyes and their body full of dust.

Though some striking out will say Why Why
and throw the blame like a spear on friends

and family, on world, man and God.
And some turning the spear to their hearts,

will almost bleed to death from their guilt
until their rage and grief growing cool

they sit with the triumph of ice and
the patience of stone and wait for love

to shift them and reveal the green life
underneath, for always the bereaved

conceal with their grief new forests, new
generations, bright colours, strong wings.

In loss the trees bear stings, and flowers
carry pain as if it were honey.

The sun is cruel. The daylight does not
understand or why does it not bring

back the dead? And God is only a
desperately personified mood

of man in his need. Grief becomes spread
like arsenic upon the warm new

bread of living: it is the slow
working of the last poison of life:

I love. In dying I kill. Such is
the law of some insects and all men.

People, animals died. Known, unknown.
Cats with wet stiff fur. Dogs that were put

to sleep in gas chambers and never
seen again. A bloated dead horse we used

to watch peeing with his immense thing
but did not really know or love. The

maggots whispered like pine trees inside
his cavernous belly, and he stank.

But these again are deaths. Absence is
the chief pain, wanting the death undone,

and when this dream is killed, the mourning
is for the dream and not for the dead

and then because dreams are within, it
is not important to move or speak

or eat, only to coffin-cradle
the lost dream in mourning without hope.

Sisters, parents…many known have died
but these are not the worst hammer blows.

We are literate in death. We learn
early the grammar, the subtleties,

vocabulary of the language;
and grief and loss are every day our

faithless teachers. We have learned that men
living may be translated as dead,

that the known dead may yet be alive.
Feeling death in a gesture, a glance,

a word spoken, we proceed to mourn
and often do not know what we mourn

or where it has gone, for burial
of love does not require stone or urn

and is its own pretence; and death of
a moment may never be confined

not even in memory but – O!
with all longing and tears may be mourned!

Loss is bewilderment, loneliness,
a vanished moment, an idea,

someone loved, maybe not even loved,
but all things once near, lost forever,

in death that uproots the familiar world
we shelter under and feed on. It

is hard to plant again with salt rain
in darkness and without hope of sun.

The Ancient Mother, a Shape of Pumice

Her precious load has dropped in her belly.
If she stays here squatting on my desk calendar
I shall have to act as midwife to her.

Her body is grey
as spring-cleaned evil or shop-soiled good.
She was burned as white heat in the volcanic fire
and now her riddled bones are set
while her body in its swollen shape submits for ever
to the black-masked highwayman calendar:

I will stand, I was born to stand here patiently.
It is you, and you, and you who must deliver.

The Bure

It is places that will not perish. I think
this now – tomorrow I may have changed my mind,
found other ways of apportioning death
between man and the earth he walks on.

I hold the Bure rising in its first
mist of water, a beginning breath
of air, unlearned in the art of flowing
though two swans try to teach it who float there.

Earth teaches it, makes its bed
beneath with weeds and stones
while the marsh orchids desperately need
its dim mirror to repair their freckles.

Confident, it surges by the mill
swirls under the bridge, widening
to the wherry-drifting reed-bordered
water where people drown in summer.

Today the Bure rises in my head;
stays, while people drown, though bones
lost years ago still give up
memories and the recently dead

hold sodden dreams in every pocket.
Today I have only the Bure, the mysterious
marsh of its beginning, that wild wind blowing
from Denmark through Cromer and the North.

Blickling Hall. The Lake. Flint Cottages.
Mountains of sugarbeet and steaming manure;
wheat and barley fields; an aluminium
sky blackened at its high edges by storm.

I hold these today in their first mist rising
across the marsh of memory
where people and places will drown; only, today
the Bure, the orchids, the two floating swans will stay.

Letter

Dear friend, the here-there emphasis is made
to keep you at a distance as I write,
to fix you, no captured human specimen
in a crowded corner of a northern world
reminding only how with spear, nail, pen,
I came your way walking from paddock to field
until at noon I fell asleep in an oak tree's shade
and waking saw not manuka and the Southern Cross
but above, Orion, and at my feet, lady-white.

A skin-thin air letter, a ninepenny stamp:
(rata or manuka or koromiko)
or words on a yellow pink green or white page
are the plan I must make, the obstacles overcome
before the public service and the plane take over my rage
to speak to you, speed-shrivel the ten thousand miles to your home
in the Midlands – fire and blotting-paper damp,
spring-feverishly mourning always the sky's loss
of sun, hanging out to dry bones stained with snow,

grey snow, last winter's fall. What else have I learned
of your city since I traced the millions
crowded on a sinking full-stop as on a doomed raft
in my first geography book and read its important name
and meaning? Small arms, bicycles, heavy drift
of smoke upward all day; diesel fumes, oil-flame, then, cultural flame
from science and music where some, not all, once burned,
survived by grafting new tissue to others who, wary at first,
soon strutted proud and warm in their smart new skin.

Meat markets, medicine, city dignitaries; an electrified line
to London from Central Station or Snow Hill.
Edgbaston. Selly Oak. A Chamberlain in office.
A Bull-Ring. Art Gallery. Dustmen. Council Flats.
Association on Association of men in business.
Undertakers, clerks, brokers; with umbrellas and top or bowler hats.
And tarnished incomes and incomes that when polished, shine.
A city of reservoirs of resigned fluoridic thirst
suckling the sweet channels flowing from the Welsh Hills.

Men silent in trains who'd never dare risk
the five-pound fine by pulling the communication cord.
Men with scientific journals; dark eyes
seeing molecules as fellow passengers

or, seeing women, tricking intelligence to tell where lies
the difference as both wrapped in genetic furs
deceive yet are worth study as a lifetime's task.
You'd think I talk of any city, not only Birmingham –
but where else into the mould are men women and bicycles poured

with equal reverence? Wheels within wheels
headlights reflectors handlebars
pumps pedals carriers hand and foot brakes,
oh and not to forget the rifles, the agricultural machines,
the bath and the kitchen sink; the articles Birmingham makes
would equip you from birth to death and after – here the touching scene
could be looked at, not through your eyes, but through locally made cinema reels,
as taking in the used label of your life, *Tear Round Here. I Am.*
You replace it with *Snip, Cover and Fold. I Was.*

My geography book is out of date. Following the new
recognition of humanity by humanity,
the miles of mountain chains everywhere
(you remember their paralysed snowcapped vertebrae)
have been made free, while rivers too have claimed their share
in the new deal, have changed their flow and no longer obey
the command of the geography book I once knew.
And now Birmingham, to me, is famous not for bicycles but for people.
It is the heart profits when facts are produced in an enlightened factory.

But it's no use. You are not there. The essence of your being
is you flow, lap at far coasts, enter rooms
invisibly to reassure me when I'm afraid
though it's not to be interpreted that therefore
I worship you, regard you as my private God.
When you're an old man you'll have a face like an apple in store,
a corner apple smelling of rain and wood, seeing
through narrow eyes nails taller than any steeple,
dead leaves and spiders set beside white scientific glooms

– does this image of you seem strange? You'll allow
it's not the usual glimpse of God; it's worse –
a theft of a separate being to complete a torn memory;
a slave-selection more frightening, tyrannical,
than is made in any past or present book of geography;
a callup of a memory-guard I've no right to call.
Death is the only guard who's willing and free Here and Now
to stay at my door, to play the memory game,
to plead too often – A bicycle? Had you not better choose a hearse?

Personal Effects

A torn plastic wallet containing a fishhook,
a rusted screw, a lucky piskie from Cornwall,
folded tattered notices of my first book,
holiday snaps of children now twice as tall
or dead, a silver watch with a broken face
marked Shockproof, though not the watch the little Levite
kept, in the hymn, in the hushed evening place
of dark temple courts and dim lamplight...

though my father's name was Samuel. Which ear must I have,
and why, I used to wonder, to hear the Word?
...a bright half-inch nail...a letter from a new love,
a tarnished bluebird brooch my mother had.
Then, as if to lure this dreary flotsam from his last high tide,
beautiful wave-skimming Greenwell's Glory, my father's pride.

Christmas

In my country Christmas is
frangipani
jacaranda
pohutukawa

is the flotsam holiday court in residence;
the king of the golden river
in swimming trunks, rubbed with sun oil,
saving the stupid who would drown outside the flags.

In my country Christmas is sun
is riches that never were rags
is plenty on the plate
is nothing for hunger who came unseen

too soon or too late;
is holiday blossom beach sea
is from me to you
is from you to me

is giving giving
in a torture of anxiety
panic of pohutukawa
jacaranda that has lost all joy.

In my country the feast
of Christmas is free;
we pay our highest price
for the lost joy
of the jacaranda tree.

L-Driver

An L-Driver through poetry,
he swerved to avoid a homily
and struck a metaphor; nothing
could save it; he drove on in shame
leaving no address and a false name.

And now his obsession is
the miraculous escape; he asks, what if
I swerve again, but having no murdered metaphor
to support me I plunge to my death over the cliff?

In a Garnet World

In a garnet world
something troubles the rock
– a rash, an itching dazzle
that will not sleep or be soothed,
a night sky of stars without sky
or night; and stars that sting.

This rock once unseen
in its river of ice, is now sick.
A man climbing cloud-high
caught human sight of it
brought to it this blood-coloured incurable
infection of light.

Unemployment

Each Tuesday at ten o'clock I go to the Employment Exchange,
fill in the form they give me, tell what I have earned
for chopping down the neighbour's tree, feeding his horse,
rescuing a silly sheep from the swamp. Sometimes, with odd jobs,
I make as much as a pound a week, but no one
offers anything permanent. The official (whom I knew at school,
a bear in the back seat) gapes at me: I'm sorry we cannot place you.

And therefore I am not placed, not in this or that. I have
a fine box of tools that I keep well-oiled. I have experience
and knowledge tied in a waiting bundle in the corner of my mind
nearest the door but no one knocks and the door is never opened.

I collect my weekly allowance. I go home,
I cuddle my wife, feed the cat,
and, for no purpose in no place, grow fat.

The Foxes

Within the purple graph of the Hokonuis, the dark
peak of Milford, my memory of Wyndham is drawn to scale.
I see the weathered grey sheep pens, their gates askew,
still standing, not used now, scattered with old sheep-dirt
like shrivelled berries of a deadly nightshade
that lead me to suppose a spreading sheep-tree grew here.
I cannot remember. The widest tree was the sky. Also,
deadly nightshade is poisonous, and sheep are not, are they?

The trains used to pass here. Wyndham station is closed now
and the railway lines like iron thorns are lifted
from their sleeper beds. The stranded station hangs
a sheltering verandah over no human traveller
for the track is overgrown with grass and it is grass, rooted on the platform,
stay-at-home, that meets only the wind passing through
with hospitality of plaintive moan and sigh
instead of the usual cup of tea and meat pie.

Sunday- and top-dressed the spring hills prosper with grass
the home paddocks with plump ewes and night-mushrooming
lambs, pink underneath, proudly declared
in the national interest, edible. The sheep, like subsidised legends, thrive,
their keepers too, but my childhood Wyndham has stayed
secure in its mutinous dream, unchanged since I knew
the railway house by the railway line and was five,
starting school, walking through long grass where the foxes lived.

INDEX OF TITLES